ROYAL BAYREUTH
A Collector's Guide

By Mary J. McCaslin

THIS BOOK IS DEDICATED TO MY HUSBAND, BOB...

His constant encouragement, and his willingness to take me "far and wide" to collect information, made the writing of this book a pleasant and worthwhile experience.

...and also to the memory of my dear mother, Frances, and step father, Mike Gurrado, who were so excited about this project, but who passed away before its completion.

TABLE OF CONTENTS

PREFACE AND ACKNOWLEDGMENTS

My first piece of Royal Bayreuth was purchased in the early 1970s at an antiques show in Indianapolis, Indiana. I still have it – a turtle creamer. Since then, I have added milk, water, and lemonade pitchers in the same pattern to make a unique and valuable set.

As collectors of this most versatile porcelain, my husband and I have enjoyed the hunt to find matching pieces or to add new pieces to our collection. Most of all, we have met many fellow collectors who share the love and excitement of collecting Royal Bayreuth (Royal Tettau), whether it is the variety of different shapes and categories of Figurals, the beautiful and numerous examples of Scenic, the ever-popular Sun Bonnet Babies, the exquisite floral designs of Rose Tapestry, and Scenic Tapestry taken from prints of famous early European artists.

I wish that I could picture all of them, but that would be impossible. If your piece or pieces are not seen in this book, it is not for lack of appreciation, but because I did not have the item to photograph. The full extent of Royal Bayreuth cannot be captured in a single book.

I have thought about a book on this subject for several years, and finally, with the encouragement of family, friends, and Antique Publications, I decided to add my small contribution to the Royal Bayreuth World. I really made this decision to begin when June Grayson, now deceased, came to my home to photograph some of our collection for an article that she was doing for a publication. She encouraged me to do this book. I have enjoyed seeing other collections and, without the kindness and generosity of many collectors who allowed their pieces to be photographed, this book would not have been possible.

My husband, Bob, has always been ready to take me wherever I needed to go. With his cooperation, this book has been a delightful experience. This project has taken us to many states to see and photograph from other collections. We traveled to Germany four times to visit the Royal Bayreuth Factory (known as Royal Tettau today). Although I have learned a great deal, there remains much I do not know. I still do not consider myself an expert on the subject.

There are so many people that I would like to thank for their contributions to this book. I hope they are pleased with the result of their kind efforts, as they entrusted me with their valuable Royal Bayreuth. My gratitude and heartfelt appreciation go to:

Ed and Helen Bailey – Missouri
Mary Baker – Ohio
Eileen Barlock – Ohio
Jim Davis – New York
June Grayson – Illinois
Tim Gaundt – Florida
Sandy and Chuck Heerhold – Illinois
Robert and Jane Larsen – Nebraska
Glenn and Jean McGuire – Washington
Walt and Judy McKee – Ohio
Arthur Milford – Florida
Qwuin O'Brien – Texas

Jolene and Harold Passow – Iowa
Dee Hooks – Illinois
Arvena and Roy Pearson – Illinois
Anna and Randy Robart – Ohio
Nancy and Mike Rublaitus – Illinois
Richard Schwartz – Missouri
Sheila Snowden – Arizona
Howard and Sally Wade – Ohio
Judy White – Michigan
John and LaVeta Woody of Woody Auction Company – Kansas

Because there was little information in English about this particular porcelain and company, I obtained books written in German. A special "thanks" must go to Ron Capers of Maryland, who translated all the research material that I could obtain. He and his wife, Noreen, accompanied us to Tettau, Germany on one occasion, and played the role of interpreter.

Alfred Herold, the Head Director of Sales at the Tettau Porcelain Factory, was my main contact in Germany. We exchanged letters over the last three years. He has been most helpful, not only in sharing information, but in being so gracious to us on our visits to the factory. We especially appreciated the chance to see the complete process of production. Jürgen Laachmann and his wife, Dagmar, were also very hospitable to us while we were in Tettau.

Walter Krautwurst of Langenqu, Germany, retired Director of Sales, Tettau Porcelain Factory (1952 - 1975) was very eager to talk to us and share his knowledge.

Oskar Wagner of Tettau, a retired school teacher who has written many papers on the porcelain of that area (Thüringer), gave us a tour of the city hall, where we were allowed to examine archives containing information on local history.

Helmut Weichler, retired Director of the Tettau factory (1968-1989), gave us an interview during our last visit to Germany. He proved to be a wealth of information because of his long association with the company. Besides being director for many years, he worked there as an apprentice from 1937.

A special "thank you" goes to previous authors, Virginia and George Salley (*Royal Bayreuth China*) and Joan and Marvin Raines (*Royal Bayreuth Figurals*). Their efforts to introduce us to the beauty and knowledge of Royal Bayreuth porcelain are greatly appreciated by all collectors and dealers. These books have served as excellent guides to help novice and advanced collectors in their search for this porcelain that we all love.

The personnel of Antique Publications have been most helpful and kind during the preparation of this book. I especially appreciated their informal, friendly manner. The photographers, Becky Van Brackel and Deana Wynn, have shown their expertise in the many beautiful photographs displayed in this book. Publisher David Richardson, also an accomplished photographer, shot some of the items pictured. Tom O'Connor edited the manuscript and Ronda Ludwig prepared the layout. Each played a big role in making this book a reality.

During the preparation of this book, I talked to many collectors and dealers. One of their main concerns was the need for accurate price information. Auction reports alone are not always reliable guides to market value. Other issues raised include: a need for explanations of pieces with more than one mark; the question of reproductions; the authenticity of many reported pieces and their production period. Through the research that I have done, I hope to shed some light on these matters.

The prices and degree of rarity stated in this book, and the accompanying value guide, should only be used as a "guide". Prices always vary from one part of the country to another. (We also know of collectors in Canada, Australia, and New Zealand.) This book does not intend to set prices. I have considered auction prices, dealer prices, personal estimates by collectors, and figures reported in the trade papers. Prices vary and are affected by the condition of a piece as well as the current demand. Purchasing from a reputable dealer is always a safe recourse.

I hope that you will enjoy the following pages of information that were written with much care and concern, because we are also collectors of this beautiful porcelain.

It is impossible to capture all shapes and colors of Royal Bayreuth in one book. If anyone has further information, on items not shown or mentioned, I would appreciate hearing from you. Please write me:

Mary J. McCaslin
272 Canterbury Drive
Danville, Indiana 46122

COMPANY HISTORY

In the beautiful Thuringia Forest of eastern Germany, the small village of Tettau is nestled among the wooded hills of Upper Franconia. The renowned porcelain factory, Königlich Priv. Porzellanfabrik Tettau, sits high on a hill overlooking the quaint village. This facility is the oldest privately owned Bavarian factory in existence today, having been founded in 1794 with a privilege granted by Friedrich Wilhelm II, King of Prussia. An historic chapel, built when the first plant was constructed, has been preserved without alteration near the factory entrance.

Privilege granted by King of Prussia, Frederich Wilhelm II who was proclaimed Emperor of Germany in the Hall of Mirrors in Versailles, and said to be one of the greatest men of the 18th century.

Today, hillside homes surround the factory and, in the wintertime, ski lovers only have to step into their backyards to enjoy this sport. The ski lift is the center of attention at this time of year, and on weekends nearly everyone hits the slopes.

"T" – The first and oldest mark used by the Royal Bayreuth factory.

The history of this region can be traced to the early 16th century. According to G. Walther, a parish vicar, "the first mention of the name Tettau was from a land grant sold to Friedrich Thuena in 1535. The overall territory was referred to as Langenawe and the village was called Tetaw." According to handwritten notes by the historian Paul Oestereicher, Tettau was a wild, desolate area at this time, with only one building that served as a kind of wooden fortress.

The settlement was further established by peasants who went into debt to purchase farmland from the Thuena landowners. Christof von Thuena expanded the main building in 1560, adding a saw mill and a tavern. This structure would serve for many years as a hunting lodge. Eventually a forge and flour mill were erected in Tettau.

In 1622, the Thuena landowners, who were indebted to authorities in Lauenstein, sold out to the Margrave of Brandenburg-Bayreuth. The hunting lodge lost its importance, and it was eventually purchased by a Pastor Hoyer who was in Langenau from 1740 until 1769. His widow sold the property in 1778 to the merchant Blank from Darmstadt. The main building was then used as a warehouse for carved wooden items which were made in Tettau and the surrounding area.

Entry to Tettau, Germany. Located in the Thuringia Forest.

The forest provided a living for most of the inhabitants. It was the source of fuel for small glassmaking operations. Other forest-dependent industries included log-raft workers and wood carvers who made, among other things, plates and water casks. These products were sent by employees of the merchant Blank through Hamburg and Nuremberg to the East and West Indies.

Pencil drawing of the main factory in Tettau, showing a larger complex than stands today (c. 1900).

Pencil drawing of new factory built (1920) in Mainleus b. Kulmbach to assist the main factory in Tettau.

An economic reversal in the area brought about the founding of the porcelain industry through the efforts of G.C.F. Greiner of Kloster Veilsdorf and the merchant, Johann Schmidt of Coburg. These gentlemen purchased the old Tettau hunting lodge from the merchant Blank and then intended to name their factory "Wilhelmsthal" (meaning William's Valley) in honor of the current king. For whatever reason, this name was not adopted, and it remained Thettau or Tettau.

In 1793, Greiner and Schmidt sought a concession to build a "true" (meaning a hard, high quality) porcelain factory in the Shauberg area of Lauenstein. This was done in a petition endorsed October 24, 1793 by the Prussian Minister Hardenberg and forwarded to the Royal Prussian Council and the Mountain Department of Bayreuth. The petition received a friendly hearing with Hardenberg because, as he stated in his endorsement, it was "well grounded and thought out."

The adviser to the Bayreuth Mountain Department at this time was Alexander von Humboldt, a well-known scientist and Royal Inspector of Mines. Therefore, the petition from Greiner and Schmidt came into the right hands. It was given favorable endorsement on November 4, 1793 by the council and the local official in Lauenstein, the bailiff Johann Valentin Fraenckel, who expressed that "there was no local objection to this undertaking." As a building site, the so-called "Swabian Meadow" of Shauberg was proposed.

On November 24, 1793, Minister Hardenberg recommended "that His Most Royal Majesty, the King, issue a special order" when next in Ansbach, to endorse the proposed porcelain factory. Fraenckel and von Humboldt supported the petition and agreed to closely monitor the negotiations

Narrow streets in the village of Tettau.

Summer hillside scene of Tettau homes.

Present-day view of Chapel built at entry to factory (c. 1800).

and report on its progress. In another recommendation letter of the same date, Hardenberg said that the king believed the investment would contribute to the improvement of local living conditions. Additional facilities were planned as well, including a brewery, malt storage building, distillery, and bakery.

The plan was good in the beginning, but soon some obstacles presented themselves. The glass makers from Kleintettau (only a few miles from Tettau) objected strongly to protect themselves from their rivals, the porcelain makers. In the records, there were several letters of dispute, hard feelings, and bitter controversy, but the porcelain entrepreneurs won out.

On March 19, 1794, it was reported that they had purchased the property. The king was notified on the completion of the factory. On December 31, 1794, he endorsed a royal decree granting them the privilege to use the term "royal" when referring to their product. Soon the porcelain factory would be known as "the most important place on the state highway" and would bring much fame to Tettau.

While Greiner's Kloster Veilsdorf factory made products with a slightly gray surface, the Tettau factory quickly succeeded in the manufacture of pure white porcelain, which the company marked with a "T". Their high quality ware soon met with much approval. Previously, the possession of "true" porcelain was reserved for royalty, but the Königl. Priv. Tettau became one of the first German factories to make its products available to a wider public. Goods were regularly dispatched into the wealthy Munsterland, still in covered wagons at that time.

Village homes with ski jump and cables for ski lift in the background. Skiing is the family winter sport.

The most important early product from the Tettau factory was tableware, especially for daily usage. Classical forms were rarely seen in Tettau porcelain. Although a rococo style was popular for some time, the company generally avoided the more complicated designs and shapes.

In addition to tableware, specialty items like doll heads and figurines were also made in the early 1800s. Regarding the figurines, a historian of this period commented that "they were not noted for their artistic tastes and were made for the common people."

Although entire dining services were manufactured, the most popular items made in Tettau during the early decades were coffee, tea, and chocolate sets. The production high point was during the 1820s and 30s, when many middle-class families obtained resplendent coffee and tea sets that would be passed down from mother to daughter.

These early marked pieces carried the "T" factory mark, mostly in red over glaze, but also in green and black over glaze, blue under glaze, and carved into the base. The tableware was made with a flat (smooth) or rippled surface and in many different sizes. The size number was usually carved into the base of the item. On pitchers and mugs, the sizes were indicated as being from 1-8.

Red, purple, black, blue, yellow, and green often served as the background colors for the tableware. Floral decorations were popular: roses, tulips, large daisies carnations, asters, or forget-me-nots—sometimes as single flowers or assembled as wreaths, garlands, or mixed bouquets.

After the turn of the century and through the trauma of World War I, the factory almost came to an untimely end. Until then, its products had been heavily exported to the United States. Because of the British blockade and a general boycott of German products, the company essentially lost its overseas market. The workers in Tettau and surrounding villages saw themselves in a dire economic situation. The factory was over stocked with merchandise and with rising debts. Production fell drastically and the plant was often idle. By mid-1915, the company had reorganized as a public stock company, and in cooperation with the workers, managed to survive.

The year 1918 brought the Tettau porcelain factory under a strong, goal-oriented leadership, which guided the company toward economic progress. In 1920, two more factories at Mainleus and Weissenbrunn-Kulmbach were added to the company. The Mainleus plant made insulators and other porcelain electrical products. However, the main factory at Tettau remained the backbone of the business. From 1919-1921, a major portion of the products were exported to America, Canada, Holland, and the Scandinavian countries.

Before World War I, the Tettau factory employed about 600 workers. In the early 1920s, there were about 480 employees. Today that number has been further reduced to 200 due to modernization.

The quality of Tettau porcelain has varied through the years, influenced by such factors as the availability of good raw materials and the turnover of managers and workers. Items were generally separated into categories based upon their quality. Depending upon their conditions as they came out of the kiln, they were usually sorted into five categories: "fractured" for cracked or broken items, "stretched" for drawn or irregularly formed pieces, "ordinary" for everyday market ware, "middle" and "fine" for better quality items or items of highest quality.

Royal Bayreuth factory with present day "logo" on the building.

When Germany was divided into east and west sectors after World War II, the factory faced many hardships due to its location on the border with East Germany. Railway communications were discontinued and a double barbed wire fence was installed through Kleintettau (next to Tettau). Railroad cars with raw materials or Tettau porcelain had to be transported 16 kilometers on low boys to the railroad station at Steinback am Wald. Tettau, being far off from the large industrial centers and so close to the border, had difficulty securing and keeping employees.

The courage to continue operating under these circumstances, while at the same time maintaining a tradition of quality, cannot be valued highly enough. Financial investments had to be made in order to rationalize and modernize obsolete factory facilities. Great effort was made to train a new generation of artisans. Some practices had to be adapted in order to be preserved. But Tettau continued to give attention to details of decoration in its manufacture of high quality porcelain.

Since the late 18th century, the Tettau factory has made a variety of decorative and functional wares. Despite the disruption caused by the two world wars, this tradition continues. Today its porcelain ranks among the most valued objects with dealers in antiques, and it is collected by many museums and private individuals.

CATEGORIES

Many categories of Tettau porcelain have been pictured and discussed in Salley's *Royal Bayreuth China* (1969) and Raines' *A Guide to Royal Bayreuth Figurals* (1974) and its Book 2 sequel (1977). Those who are not fortunate enough to have a copy of these earlier books will, I hope, especially welcome the summary of information in this chapter.

Although more than 1300 plus items are illustrated in this book, I want to say again that it is impossible to show or describe every kind of figural, scenic, or tapestry that was produced during the years of production from about 1885 up to the start of World War I. I have tried to show a sampling of each category to present a guide to help collectors in their search.

Furthermore, it is difficult to measure rarity in the description of each piece, because what may be scarce in one area may be more available in another. Some items, such as the Santa Claus figural and some tapestry pieces, are admittedly harder to find, and their higher prices reflect this fact.

The Royal Bayreuth products can be found in a tapestry (linen) finish, a high gloss finish, or a satin (mother-of-pearl) finish. The tapestry effect was obtained by wrapping the item in a coarse, linen-type cloth. The material burned away during the firing, leaving a texture similar to needlepoint tapestry. The decorations, such as a portrait, scenic, or floral, were then applied.

Kathy Wojciechowski, authority on Nippon (Japanese) porcelain, wrote in the *New York-Pennsylvania Collector* (November 14, 1992) that Nippon produced some tapestry items in imitation of Royal Bayreuth in the years 1891-1911. Most of these items have Nippon's blue maple leaf mark and they were not made in great quantities.

Tapestry pieces are desired by most Royal Bayreuth collectors, and they are hard to obtain. From talking to numerous collectors, I believe that the Rose Tapestry, which consists of several colors and species of roses, is probably the most obtainable. These were designed by the artists in the factory and then made into a decal. Christmas Rose, Violets, Forget-me-nots, and Japanese Chrysanthemums are other popular choices. A silver or black rose tapestry creamer and basket shown in this book are the only ones reported in this unusual color to date.

There are also many beautiful scenic and portrait pieces in the Tapestry category, such as: The Cavalier Musicians; The Peasant Musicians; The "Toaster" Cavalier or Tavern Scene; The "Bathers" (or Nudes); Colonial attired people; The Muff Lady; The Shawl Lady; The Lady with the Horse; Highland Cattle, Sheep and Goats; The Peering Lady (hand shielding eyes); Hunt Scenes; Farm Scenes; Portrait Ladies; Swans; Castle and Water Scenes; The Polar Bears; and others. Some of the scenes were taken from prints of famous European artists. Tapestry and Scenic also may be found in various shapes and sizes of plates, bowls, pitchers, picture frames, toothpick holders, salt and pepper shakers, tea pots and sets, humidors, vases, ashtrays, candlestick holders, cracker jars, baskets, mustard pots, nut sets, sugar and creamers, hair receivers, various covered pieces, bells, desk sets, dresser sets, hatpin holders, dresser trays, clocks, shoes, planters, wall pockets, match holders, mugs, miniature childs' furniture (sofa and chairs), and others.

The **Animal, Bird,** and **Fish** pieces are found in forms from the domestic dog and cat to the exotic lion and tiger. These decorations are mostly portrayed on pitchers, covered pieces, humidors, hatpin holders, ashtrays, match holders, salt shakers, candlestick holders, and other novelty pieces. The Leopard and Tiger have only been reported as creamers and are considered among the rarities, along with the Rabbit, Squirrel, Mouse and Kangaroo, in the figural category. The Turtle and the Big Mouth Fish are shown in four pitcher sizes. The very colorful Butterfly is found in three different molds: the open wing, the closed wing, and the perched version. The Ladybug and Beetle are the same mold. Spots have been added to designate the Ladybug. A "Cat–handle" (black or white) or a "Parrot–handle" (red or white), may be seen on pitchers of red, white, green, or ecru (tan).

The **Art Nouveau Lady** is a beautiful and graceful form. Art Nouveau was a movement of the late 19th and early 20th century, characterized by curvilinear designs styled from nature. The trend of the times is often shown in the lady's movements. This graceful category is very sought after in pitchers, dresser sets, toothpick holders, vases, bowls, covered pieces, candlestick holders, baskets, and other decorative pieces.

The **Clown** characters are found in both male and female forms. Pitchers, dresser sets, covered pieces, bowls, candlestick holders, humidors, match holders, ashtrays, and other novelty pieces can be found in this colorful and unique motif. Yellow, green and white satin finish are a little harder to find than the usual red.

Corinthian or **Classic** are presented in the Scenic category. They display graceful, elaborate Roman or Greek characters, usually with a border of an Acanthus leaf, which is a thistle-like plant found in the Mediterranean region. This motif was used on the capitals of Corinthian columns. Many pieces are found in the form of pitchers, mugs, loving cups, vases of all sizes, covered pieces, candlestick holders, bowls, and many other novelty pieces. A beautiful variety of colors are in red, black, green, and yellow.

Devil and Cards is a very bright and showy series depicted by various playing cards (decals) with a red devil forming the handle of many pieces or as an added adornment. Many sizes and shapes are found in this decorative pattern. Included are pitchers, covered pieces, humidors, salt shakers, plates, mugs, toothpick holders, ashtrays, and other novelty pieces such as a devil/dice cube. Some of these items were reissued for a brief time after World War II. The Raines state that these were the only figurals to use transfers or decals. (See the chapter on marks for more information.)

A **Red Devil** (solid color) is also found in pitchers, toothpick holders, ashtrays, and a demi-cup. There may be others, but I am not aware of them.

The **Elk**, is a popular series found in various forms to offer the collector a wide choice. A complete collection of elk makes a fine display. Pitchers, covered pieces, humidors, dishes (such as celery or relish), candlestick holders, toothpick holders, mugs, planters, inkwells, ashtrays, and even a "toddy set" are available.

Fruit figurals provide us with a category of many colorful, collectible shapes and sizes. The ones known are almonds, apples, cherries, grapes, lemons, oranges, peaches, pears, pineapples, plums, strawberries, and watermelons. They may be found in four sizes of pitchers (lemonade, water, milk, and creamer), plates, tea sets, covered pieces, vases, cracker jars, salt shakers, mustard pot with spoon, and others. The beautiful array of showy colors are a plus to a collection.

The **Flower** category consists of the anemone (a member of the buttercup family with cup-shaped flowers that are usually white, pink, red, or purple), chrysanthemum, clover, geranium, orchid, oxalis (a five-parted flower in white, pink, red, or yellow), pansy, poinsettia, poppy, rose, and sunflower. The rose, pansy, and poppy groups have more reported pieces such as pitchers (various sizes), cracker jars, tea sets, covered pieces, bowls, plates, hatpin holders, chocolate sets, candlestick holders, salt shakers, and vases. The other flowers are more limited and have been seen in pitchers, hatpin holders, and an occasional demi-cup and saucer. A tea strainer in the anemone and the oxalis can be found.

Leaf patterns are from the maple, oak or holly. Colors are green, variegated autumn array, and white satin finish.

The **Lobster** and **Lobster and Leaves** are fairly common series found in pitchers, covered pieces, bowls, plates, salt shakers, ashtrays, cracker jars, etc. Dates and names have been applied to some to serve as souvenirs of a certain locale or occasion. Red pieces are most frequently found, but they can also be seen in orchid/white satin finish.

The **Shell** has numerous shapes and sizes in the figural category. Some have a satin finish and others have a shiny luster. A gold overlay has been applied to a select few. One variation of the shell is the "spiky" exterior, resembling the Murex (a snail with a rough, shiny shell). Another is the "Nautilus Shell" which is a many-chambered, spiral shell with a pearly interior (sometimes painted in a black decor). Pitchers, cracker jars, humidors, plates, bowls, candlestick holders, covered pieces, tea sets, toothpick holders, and other novelty pieces give collectors a wide variety to hunt for. Also included is a **Spiky Shell with a Coral Handle** or a **Shell with a Lobster Handle**, reported in pitchers.

People figurals are few and limited to special categories, which include the **Bellringer** (town crier who gave public announcements), **Coachman** (driver of a coach in early days), and the **Lamplighter** (the man who lit and extinguished gas street lamps). These are depicted in pitchers, humidors, toothpick holders, and hatpin holders. The **Milkmaid, Girl with Basket or Pitcher**, and **Monks** are available in small pitchers.

Santa Claus pieces are a very sought after category and seen in pitchers (lemonade, water, milk, and creamers), tall and low candlestick holders, hat pin holders, humidors, candy dishes, ashtrays, match holders (with striker on pack), hanging match holders, and a wall plaque or vase (full figure). Besides the traditional red, they may also be found in green or brown.

Scenic pieces make up a very large category with many divisions. I will not expound in great detail on this group that has such a wide assortment of collectible Royal Bayreuth. There are numerous scenes such as Arabs in a desert setting, Barnyard scenes, Butterfly (embossed) motif, the Cavalier Musicians, The "Toaster" Cavalier (or Tavern Scene), The Bathers (Nudes), the Chambermaid or Candle Girl, Colonial attired people, Cow in Pasture, Donkey/Boy, Dutch scene, Fighting Cocks, the Fisherman, Fisherman/Canoe, Flower with Metal filigree top, the Fox, Fruit scenes, Harvest Girls, Highland Cattle, Sheep or Goats, Horsemen and women scenes, Hunt scenes, the Lawyer, Mountain Goat in the Snow, the Peasant Musicians, the Penguin, Roosters, the Stork, Witches Brew, Work Horses, and others . The Brittany Girl, symbolizing the British Empire, is popular with its blue border. These various series are found in many forms from pitchers to novelty pieces.

The **Sun Bonnet Babies** is a series by itself. This popular pattern was created by Bertha L. Corbett, an American artist. It appeared on German porcelain at the turn of the century. She characterized children doing daily chores and other activities such as Fishing (Sunday), Washing (Monday), Ironing (Tuesday), Mending (Wednesday), Scrubbing (Thursday), Sweeping (Friday), Baking (Saturday). They are portrayed on various forms with a high gloss finish. Some of them are pitchers of various sizes, tea sets, plates, candlestick holders, desk sets, ashtrays, tea tiles, dresser sets, baskets, bells, hat-pin holders, covered pieces and even a sabot (Dutch shoe). Also in this category, we find the **Beach Babies**, **Snow Babies**, **Jack and Jill**, **Little Miss Muffet**, **Babes in the Woods**, **Girl with Dog**, **Little Bo Peep**, **Mary Had a Little Lamb**, **Little Boy Blue**, and **Jack and the Beanstalk**.

The **Tomato** figural, only reported in its true red color, was produced in great quantity and is, therefore, more common and easier to find. It makes a very attractive collection, as there are so many pieces in various shapes and sizes. Pitchers, tea sets, covered pieces, bowls, plates, cracker jars, candlestick holders, and other novelty pieces make up some of the great variety.

Lettuce Leaves, **Chili Pepper**, **Pepper**, **Celery**, **Cucumber**, **Radish**, and **Corn** are among the other vegetables that are found. Bowls, plates, hatpin holders, salt shakers and some dishes are seen in this category. The Lettuce Leaf plates are often used as underplates for the tomato pieces.

There are several **Shoes** that have been seen and reported in many different styles and colors, from turn-of-the-century high and lace button shoes to oxfords, low cuts, strap shoes, slippers and others. They were usually of high gloss finish with the exception of those with a tapestry finish decorated in floral or scenic. Some are seen (in this book) to be pin cushions.

Four sizes of pitchers are found in the figural category. They may be labeled as lemonade, water, milk, and creamer. At the present time, I have seen this set in the figural Apple, Big Mouth Fish, Santa Claus, and the Turtle. If readers know of others, I would appreciate having this information for future use. My address is listed on page 7.

MARKS AND "TIDBITS" OF INFORMATION

Royal Bayreuth marks have varied throughout the years, in part because each new manager would change the crest in some way to show a distinction for the tenure in which he held this position.

After watching the process of manually stamping the pieces with a rubber stamp or applying the paper decal mark, it is understandable why some of the marks on finished products may have a blurred or smudged appearance. It is possible for the decal or the rubber stamp, to slip during its application. A trace of a mark or signature is always reassuring of the authenticity to some collectors, but many pieces do not carry this identification and are still as valuable and collectible. A seasoned collector soon can spot a piece of Royal Bayreuth from afar without picking it up to check the mark.

Marks such as "KI, BAVARIA" are added marks by companies that have purchased the Royal Bayreuth to use as advertising or souvenir pieces by adding their logo to the piece. (e.g. **MW** for Montgomery Ward, and others).

Since 1880, Tettau has used special marks for export pieces. In Europe, they used "Kgl. priv Tettau".

The Devil and Cards reproductions were produced in 1946 - 1949. These were imported to the United States and never to England. They were marked Royal Bayreuth U. S. Zone. Numbers on the piece designate the painter or artist (e.g.: f .i. no. 23 means artist, Anton Meier a.s.o.). The number may also denote the decoration (e.g.: f.i.2214 means "black rose"). The weight of authentic pieces in the same shape and line may vary. This is because they are hand-crafted, cast items.

Tettau did not produce figurines. However, it is known (according to the factory) that about 1870, the company "Schneider, Gräfenthal" (which is located near Tettau) used the Tettau mark illegally for their figurines. These were exported to the United States.

The U.S. Zone mark (added to the original stamp) was a duty for all pieces that were produced from 1945 – 1949. Germany was separated into four zones and Bavaria belonged to the U.S. Zone until 1949. This was the foundation of the Federal Republic of Germany.

The factory reported that plain white pieces or blanks were exported to New Zealand from 1900 - 1920. The decorations were applied there by a New Zealand artist, "Dixon". This signature appears on some of the "Cavalier Musician" pieces.

A New Zealand collector related an interesting story that has been passed down. Two beautiful large rose vases were displayed in a hotel in Nelson, New Zealand. This occurred in 1927, during a visit by the Duke and Duchess of York. (He was the future George VI of Great Britain.) The vases were 7½ inches high and 19 inches in circumference, stamped with the Royal Bayreuth blue mark. They were inscribed "Hand-painted, Roses, Her Majesty (in red)". It is believed that these pieces were made especially for the royal visit.

"Michielotto" is an Italian customer of the present day Tettau factory. Sun Bonnet Babies was reproduced for them from about 1975-1980. The pieces are well marked, showing that they are a limited edition by the original manufacturer and the year they were made. The "Michielotto" stamp is included to insure collectors that this is not the original piece. "Kern Collectibles" is also a private company that purchased and distributed the Sun Bonnet Babies series in 1981. These are also well marked to not confuse the buyer.

These marks are attributed to the Königlich Priv. Porzellanfabrik Tettau GmbH. (Königlich Priv. Porcelain Factory Co.) – 1794 – Present Time . . . .

#1 – Mark – 1794 - 1885
    Blue – Underglaze . . .

T.

#2 – Mark – 1794 - 1885
    Blue – Underglaze . . .

T.

#3 – Mark – 1794 - 1885
    Blue – Underglaze . . .

T.

T.

#4 – Mark – 1794 - 1885
    Blue – Underglaze . . .

T.

#5 – Mark – 1794 - 1885
    Blue – Underglaze . . .

#6 – Mark – 1866 - 1887
    Gold – Overglaze . . .

#7 – Mark – um (around) 1887 - 1902
    Stamped
    Green or Blue – Underglaze . . .

#8 – Mark – um (around) 1900 . . .

#9 – Mark – After 1900
    Stamped
    Green or Blue – Underglaze
    Blue, gray or Gold – Overglaze after 1902 . . .

#10- Mark – After 1900
    Stamped
    Blue or Green – Underglaze
    Other Colors – Overglaze . . .

#11- Mark – After 1900
    Blue or Green – Underglaze . . .

#12 – Mark – 1919
    Green . . .

#13 – Mark – 1946 - 1949
    U.S. Zone . . .

#14 – Mark – 1946 - 1949
    Found on 1946 reissues in green, U.S.Zone . . .

#15 – Mark – After 1900
    Green and Black
    Blue circa 1900 . . .

#16 – Mark – After 1900 . . .

#17 – Mark – After 1900
     Blue or Green . . .

#18 – Mark – After 1968
     Blue or Green . . .

#l9 –   Mark – After 1968
     Green – Underglaze
     Gold, Blue, or Red – Overglaze . . .

#20 – Mark – After 1968
     Green Underglaze . . .

#21 – Mark – After 1968
     Blue (and possible other colors) . . .

#22 – Mark – 1968 – Present
     (Atelier = Studio) . . .

REGISTERED – Denoting registration . . .

"Deponiert" – May be found alone or on a marked piece. This (according to Mr.
or "Depose" Weichler, past Directory of Tettau) is to assure the buyer that the
mold is in tact and may be re-ordered.

ADDED MARKS FOUND ON ROYAL BAYREUTH

The floral raised mark below can be with the "Blue Mark" or without. I have only seen it on the figural Pear. The Goblin and Josephine marks are examples of marks that have been added to special
order items by other companies. These pieces also had the Royal Bayreuth mark.

FACTORY OWNERSHIP

1794 - 1852 – George Christian Friedmann Griener
1852 - 1866 – Ferdinand Klaus
1866 - 1879 – Wilhelm Sontag and Karl Birkner
1879 - 1902 – Karl Birkner and L. Maisel
1897 - Factory was destroyed by fire and new factory was
built on the same site – 1897 - 1915.
1915 - Open Stock Company

Today (1993) the factory is owned by Mr. Christian Sellmann Wieden and directed by Mr. Werner
Weiherer.

INTERVIEW WITH PAST DIRECTOR OF THE TETTAU FACTORY

After visiting several public and college libraries, I concluded that there was little or no information on Tettau or Royal Bayreuth Porcelain printed in English. In books and articles on porcelain, the Tettau factory was only mentioned briefly as one of many factories in the German Bavarian country.

After corresponding with Alfred Herold, Head Sales Director of the factory, we decided to see for ourselves the beautiful country and factory that produced our Royal Bayreuth. We made four trips to Germany to gather information. The factory personnel, town archives, and books on Royal Bayreuth became my main sources. The books were written in German, so I had to have them translated. On my last visit, I talked to Helmut Weichler, who had been director of the factory from 1968 until his retirement in 1989. He spoke only German, so Mr. Herold served as our translator. I hope my recollection of our fascinating visit will be interesting to others as it was to me.

Helmut Weichler

Meeting the past director of the Tettau factory was a pleasure and we felt very privileged for him to share his valuable time and knowledge with us. We sat at a table in the factory show room, with Mr. Herold as our translator. Even though I did not understand the language, the pride and enthusiasm of his association with this unique porcelain showed in his face and there was excitement in the tone of his voice. He has been an important influence on Royal Bayreuth (Royal Tettau) for over 50 years. He still resides in Tettau since his retirement. With a large smile on his face, he said that he was first introduced to the porcelain business at the tender age of six. His mother and father were employed in the factory at that time. There were no "baby sitters," so he was taken to work with his mother and sat in a chair most of the day, watching the process which would later become his livelihood. He started his apprenticeship in 1937. His career was interrupted by World War II. Serving in the German Army, he was wounded and captured by the Russians at the age of eighteen. After spending four years in a Russian prison camp, he was released and returned to Tettau. He resumed his career in the Tettau Factory, working his way up the corporate ladder to become director in 1968.

Being so closely associated with the porcelain industry for so long, he is probably one of the best versed experts today. He held an important role in the transformation from hand production to the machine age. He related enlightening stories about the old production, as he knew it, and a few personal stories that took place during his tenure with the Tettau factory. For example, he made the interesting point that the popular Devil and Card series symbolized that "all gamblers were not in control of their lives and had fallen victim to the wiles or deceitful tricks of the Devil." He verified that all ledgers, journals, and records at Tettau were destroyed in the fire of 1897. Because I have searched and inquired many places about Royal Bayreuth, I truly believe there is very little written about this company. This fire leveled the factory to the ground as it existed in that day. All of the pieces that are shown in the archive room of the factory today have been donated or bought by the factory.

According to Mr. Weichler, exporting to the United States did not start until about 1870. The United States remained Royal Bayreuth's leading importer until 1915.

He further indicated that during his lifetime there was no production of scenic, tapestry, or figural Royal Bayreuth. The exception was the re-issue of "Devil and Cards," U.S. Zone. These were made for a private company and marked on the bottom of the item "1905-1985" under the glaze. There was also a re-issue of the Sun Bonnet Babies for an Italian Exporter in the 1970s. These were marked "Michiellotto" and were a limited edition.

Since his information was drawn mostly from memory, he was very careful to relate those facts that he knew to be true. The tapestry and scenic production covered the years 1890-1915 and figural production approximately 1900-1915. This information had been gathered from co-workers and his parents who had been employed at the factory before 1915. To his best knowledge, there are no records of exact dates for the production of these categories.

Following World War I, the United States was again the leading importer for Royal Bayreuth and continued as such until World War II. The director at that time, Max Wunderlich, traveled to the United States by steamer to see the World Heavyweight Championship fight between Joe Louis and Max Schmeling in 1938. He visited various importers on the East Coast of the United States. The outlet stores for Royal Bayreuth at that time included Tiffany's, Macy's, and Bloomingdales, all of New York. The leading Canadian outlet was Miller Brothers in Toronto, Canada.

Before 1914, Royal Tettau had their own import house in the United States. From 1960 into the 1990s, Wittur Co. of Evanston, Illinois has been the exclusive importer. There was a strong market in the U.S.A. from 1946 until the less expensive porcelain from Japan captured the American market. Eventually the small European porcelain companies were not able to compete.

In 1978, a director of a large Berlin museum asked Mr. Weichler to explain the "linen or tapestry" process, because there was no other on the market like it. His reply was a gracious, but firm, "It's a secret." Although he explained, in general, the process to us, I feel his 1978 reply is the best for collectors of today also. The process remains Tettau's secret and, apart from some Japanese attempts at imitation, it remains a lost art in porcelain production. I know of no other that compares to this beautiful example of fine porcelain. The portraits displayed on many pieces are from famous European artists of the 17th and 18th centuries. The United States and Canada were the major markets for tapestry with the greatest amount going to the United States from 1890-1915.

The interview was a memorable experience as Mr. Weichler and Mr. Herold were eager to share their knowledge and love of the Royal Bayreuth that we have collected for over 20 years. If you should go to Germany, do not pass up the opportunity to visit the village of Tettau.

DESCRIPTION OF ITEMS ILLUSTRATED IN COLOR

PAGE 33

Row 1:   **1.** Charger Plate: Donkey / Boy (Farm Scene Background) – 13"D
   2. Tankard: Work Horse (Farm Scene Background) – 11½" H (5qt)
   3. Charger Plate: Work Horse (Farm Scene Background) – 13"D

Row 2:   **4.** Chocolate Pot - (with Decorative Lid): Donkey – 8½"H
   5. Wall Plaque: Work Horse with Gold Scroll Border – 10"D
   6. Lemonade Pitcher: Work Horse (Farm Scene Background) – 8"H

Row 3:   **7.** Milk Pitcher: Black Cow Scene with Plain Green Bottom – 5"H
   8. Picture Frame: Lady Riding Horse /Man & Woman Watching – 8¼"L x 6"W
   9. Milk Pitcher: Cow – 4¾"H
   10. Creamer: Work Horse (Farm Scene Background) – 4"H
   11. Milk Pitcher: Work Horse (Farm Scene Background) – 5"H

Row 4:   **12.** Bowl: Donkey / Boy, Child Size – 1½"H
   13. Match Holder: Work Horse, Coal Hod Shape – 3"H
   14. Teapot: Work Horse, Child Size – 3½"H
   15. Creamer: Work Horse, Child Size – 3"H
   16. Salt Shaker: Work Horse, (Farm Scene Background) – 3½"H

PAGE 34

Row 1:   **17.** Humidor (with Lid): Skiff with Sail and Windmill, Blue – 6"H
   18. Charger Plate: Skiff with Sail and Windmill, Blue – 13"D
   19. Vase: Skiff with Sail, Brown – 8"H

Row 2:   **20.** Milk Pitcher: Chambermaid with Candle, (or Candle Lady) – 6¼"H
   21. Milk Pitcher: Highland Cattle – 4½"H
   22. Milk Pitcher: Highland Cattle, Yellow/Brown – 4½"H
   23. Milk Pitcher: Skiff with Sail, Double Handled, Brown – 5"H

Row 3:   **24.** Toothpick Holder: Arab, Three-Handled – 3"H
   25. Coffee Pot: Miniature (Child), Hunt Scene – 3"H
   26. Scuttle Mug: Goose Girl – 3½"H
   27. Creamer: Dog, (Farm Scene Border), Corset Shape – 4"H
   28. Creamer: Penguin, Yellow – 3"H

Row 4:   **29.** Pin Tray: Cavalier Musicians (Mandolin) and Cork (sometimes signed "Dixon") – 4¾"L x 3½"W
   30. Ink Well: Grazing Cow, (Three-Piece) – 4½"H
   31. Ashtray: Frog and Bee – 5¾"L x 3½"W

PAGE 35

Row 1:   **32.** Plate: Peasant Musicians, (Violin and Horn) – 9"D
   33. Vase: Peasant Musicians, (Violin and Horn) – 9"H
   34. Plate: Peasant Musicians, (Mandolin) – 9"D

Row 2:   **35.** Bowl: Fruit (Grapes) – 10½"D
   36. Bowl: Rose Tapestry, Shell and Leaf Mold – 10½"D
   37. Bowl: Muff Lady – 10½"D

Row 3:   **38.** Cracker Jar (with Lid): Poppy, Red – 4¼"W x 6¼"H
   39. Vase: Castle by the Lake, Gold Trim – 5¾"H

40. Plate: Triple-Pink, Rose Tapestry, Shell and Leaf Mold – 5¾"D

41. Nappy: The Hunt (Horseman with Dogs), Rolled Edge, Triangle Shape – 6"L

Row 4: **42.** Toothpick Holder: Floral, (Three-Handled Wedding Cup) – 2¼"H

43. Creamer: Goose Girl, (Three-Handled Wedding Cup) – 3½"H

44. Creamer: Skiff with Sail, Black – 2½"H

45. Relish: Swans on Lake, Handled – 5½"W x 6"L

46. Toothpick Holder: Horse-Woman with Dogs – 2½"H

PAGE 36

Row 1: **47.** Vase: Brittany Women, Souvenir Signed "Niagara Falls, Canada" – 7"H

48. Salt and Pepper Shakers: Rose – 3¼"H

49. Water Pitcher: Rose With Rose Decor Inside – 7¾"H

50. Salt and Pepper Shakers: Brittany Women – 3¼"H

51. Candlestick Holder: Brittany Women, Tall Size – 6¼"H

Row 2: **52.** Teapot: Brittany Women, Green Shades – 3"H x 6½"W

53. Teapot: Boy and Turkeys, Decorated Lid – 4½"H x 7"W

54. Teapot: Rooster and Hen, Brown – 3¼"H x 7"W

55. Teapot: Muff Lady – 4½"H x 7"W

Row 3: **56.** Teapot: Brittany Women, Blue – 3½"H x 6¾"W

57. Candlestick Holder: Brittany Women (Shield) – 4½"H

58. Candlestick Holder: Brittany Women, Medium Size – 4¼"H

Row 4: **59.** Hair Receiver: Brittany Women, Footed – 2½"H x 4¼"W

60. Candlestick Holder: Brittany Women, Low, Handled – 1¾"H

61. Nappy: Brittany Women, Leaf Shape – 6½"L x 6"W

PAGE 37

Row 1: **62.** Lemonade Pitcher: The Chase (Hounds and Stag in Stream,) Red Bottom – 6¾"H

63. Vase: Brittany Girls (Farm Scene Top Border) – 8"H

64. Chocolate Pot: Work Horse (Farm Scene Background) – 8"H

65. Tankard: Wheat Girl with Chickens, – 10¾"H

Row 2: **66.** Candlestick Holder: Tall, Toaster Cavalier (Stein Extended), Green – 6"H

67. Candlestick Holder: Low, Toaster Cavalier (Stein Extended), Green – 2¼"H x 6"L

68. Loving Cup: Corinthian with Acanthus Leaf Border, Three-Handled, Black – 4¼"H

69. Candlestick Holder: Black Cow – 6"L x 2¼"H

70. Vase: Cow, (Brown and White, Facing East) – 5"H

Row 3: **71.** Ashtray: Hunter with Dog in Tree, Square shape – 5¼"W

72. Plate: Arab on Brown Horse – 6"D

73. Hat Pin Holder: Arab on Brown Horse, Round Base – 4¾"H

74. Milk Pitcher: Arab on White Horse - 4"H

75. Plate: Arab on White Horse – 6"D

76. Candy Dish: Dutch Girl (Hexagon Shape) – 4¾"W

Row 4: **77.** Mint or Nut Dish Set: Bowl: Large Pedestal Master – 5½"H x 2½"D; Bowls: Small – 1"H x 2½"D; Scenes: Highland Sheep, Donkey/Man, Donkey/Boy, Black Cow, Cow

PAGE 38

Row 1: **78.** Plate: Corinthian (or Classic) with Acanthus Leaf Border, Roman Figures, Red – 9½"D

79. Loving Cup: Corinthian (or Classic) with Acanthus Leaf, Roman Figure, Three-Handled, Red – 4½"H

80. Creamer: Corinthian (or Classic) with Acanthus Leaf, Roman Figure, Red – 4¼"H

81. Candlestick Holder: Highland Sheep, Red – 5¼"H

82. Humidor (with Lid): Cottage by the Waterfall (Rhineland Scene) – 7"H

Row 2: **83.** Creamer: Corinthian (or Classic) with Acanthus Leaf, Yellow, Roman Figure – 4"H

84. Creamer: Corinthian (or Classic) with Acanthus Leaf, Yellow – 3¾"H

85. Creamer: Corinthian (or Classic) with Acanthus Leaf, Black – 4¼"H

86. Sugar (with Lid): Corinthian (or Classic) with Acanthus Leaf, Black – 3"H

87. Creamer: Corinthian (or Classic) with Acanthus Leaf, Roman Figure, Black – 3¾"H

88. Teapot: Corinthian (or Classic) with Acanthus Leaf, Roman Figure, Black – 3"H x 7"W,

Row 3: Tea Set: Iridescent Shell with Gold Trim

89. Cup and Saucer: Iridescent Shell with Gold Trim – Cup 2"H, Saucer 4¾"D

90. Sugar (with Lid): Iridescent Shell with Gold Trim – 3"H

91. Creamer: – Iridescent Shell with Gold Trim – 3"H

92. Teapot: – Iridescent Shell with Gold Trim – 3¾"H x 7"W

Row 4: **93.** Bud Vase: Colonial People with Dog, Miniature, with Handle – 3"H

94. Match Holder: Indian Design (with Strike Area) – 2½"H

95. Match Holder: Lady Riding Horse/Man and Woman Watching (with Strike Area) – 2½"H

96. Double Bud Vase: Highland Cattle, Miniature, with Handle – 3"H

PAGE 39
Row 1: **97.** Vase: Tapestry, Rare Japanese Chrysanthemum, Reverse Cone Shape – 8½"H

98. Bowl: Peacock, Shell and Leaf Mold, – 10½"D

99. Cake Plate: Arab on White Horse, Open Handled – 10½"D

100. Tankard: Arab on Brown Horse – 9¼"H

Row: 2 **101.** Plate: The Hunter with One Dog – 10½"D

102. Bowl: Peasant Musicians (Violin and Horn) – 9½"D

103. Plate: The Fishermen (Two Men in Boat) – 10½"D

Row 3: **104.** Milk Pitcher: Skiff with Sail, Double Handled – 5"H

105. Milk Pitcher: Peacock – 5¼"H

106. Milk Pitcher: Hunter with Dogs – 5¼"H

107. Candlestick Holder: Arab on White Horse – 4¼"H

108. Candlestick Holder: Hunter with Dogs – 5¼"H

109. Water Pitcher: Polar Bear, Blue – 6½"H

Row 4: **110.** Toothpick Holder: White Rose, Tapestry, Handled – 2½"H

111. Toothpick Holder: Pink Border Rose, Tapestry, Three Holed – 2¾"H

112. Mustard Pot (with Lid): The Fishermen (Two Men) – 2¾"H

113. Creamer: Lone Fisherman (Standing in Boat) – 3¾"H

114. Hanging Match Holder: Lone Fisherman (Standing in Boat) – 4¼"H

PAGE 40
Row 1: **115.** Milk Pitcher: Babes in the Woods, Cobalt – 4½"H

116. Teapot: Babes in the Woods, Cobalt - 3"H x 6¾"W

117. Sugar with Lid: Babes In the Woods, Cobalt – 2½"H x 5½"W

118. Vase: Babes In the Woods, Crying Child, Cobalt – 4¼"H

Row 2: **119.** Babies Hair Receiver: Nursery Rhymes, Sand Babies – 3" H x 4"W

120. Vase: Babes in the Woods, Miniature, Handled, Cobalt – 3"H

121. Vase: Babes in the Woods, Miniature, Cobalt – 3"H

122. Bell: Babes in the Woods, (One Girl) - Cobalt – 3"H x 2½"D

123. Creamer: Babes in the Woods, Cobalt – 3 1/2"H

124. Milk Pitcher: Nursery Rhymes, Little Jack Horner – 5"H

Row 3: **125.** Bell: Goose Girl (All with Clappers) – 3"H x 2½"D

126. Bell: Highland Sheep (5) – 3"H x 2½"D

127. Bell: Lady on Horse with Man & Woman Watching – 3"H x 2½"D

128. Bell: Work Horses (2) – 3"H x 2½"D

129. Bell: Hunt Scene (Three dogs) – 3"H x 2½"D

130. Bell: Cattle Scene (3) – 3"H x 2½"D

131. Bell: Man with Sickle and Chickens – 3"H x 2½"D

Row 4: **132.** Bell: Nursery Rhymes, Jack and Jill – 3"H x 2½"D

133. Bell: Sun Bonnet Babies, Fishing – 3"H x 2½"D

134. Bell: Peasant Musicians, (Violin and Horn) – 3"H x 2½"D

135. Bell: Pheasant – 3"H x 2½"D

136. Bell: Mule and Two Men – 3"H x 2½"D

137. Bell: Corinthian with Acanthus Leaf Border, Black – 3"H x 2½"D

138. Bell: Muff Lady – 3"H x 2½"D

PAGE 41

Row 1: **139.** Plate: Nursery Rhyme, Jack and Jill – 7¼"D

140. Cake Plate: Little Boy Blue, (Open-Handled) – 10½"D

141. Plate: Little Bo-Peep – 7¼"D

142. Plate: Little Bo-Peep, Gold Trim – 7¼"D

Row 2: **143.** Plate: Girl with Dog – 7"D

144. Plate: Ring Around Rosey – 6"D

145. Plate: Sand Babies (or Beach Babies) – 5¾"D

146. Plate: Little Boy Blue – 6"D

147. Candy Dish: Little BoPeep (Spade Shape) – 4¾"L

Row 3: **148.** Plate: Sunbonnet Babies, Fishing – 7¼"D

149. Bowl: Sunbonnet Babies, Fishing – 5¾"D

150. Bowl: Sunbonnet Babies, Fishing – 5"D

151. Bowl: Sunbonnet Babies, Ironing – 5¾"D

152. Candlestick Holder: Sunbonnet Babies, Mopping (Shield) – 4¾"H

Row 4: **153.** Candy Dish: Little Jack Horner, Leaf Shape – 5"L

154. Vase: Dutch Boy and Girl, Handled, Miniature – 3"H

155. Saucer: (Three) Little Girls with Dog – 3¾"D

156. Cup: Children, Teeter-Totter – 2"H

157. Cup: Snow Babies, Sledding – 2¼"H

158. Saucer: Snow Babies, Ice Play – 5¼"D

159. Candy Dish: Snow Babies, Ice Play, Leaf Shape – 5"L

PAGE 42

Row 1: **160.** Wall Plaque: Turkeys, with Gold Scroll Border – 11½"D

161. Candlestick: Goose Girl – 5½"H

162. Charger Plate: Goose Girl – 13"D

Row 2: **163.** Humidor: Man with Sickle and Chickens, Decorative Lid – 5½"H

164. Milk Pitcher: Sunbonnet Babies, Fishing, Pinched Spout – 4¼"H

165. Milk Pitcher: Sunbonnet Babies, Fishing – 4¾"H

166. Milk Pitcher: Sunbonnet Babies, Fishing, Light Blue – 4"H

167. Lemonade Pitcher: Lady and Chickens – 6½"H

Row 3: **168.** Stamp Box (with Lid): Little Bo Peep – 5"L x 1½"W

169. Brush: Girl with Dog – 3" x 2"H

170. Letter Holder: Ring Around Rosey – 6"H x 4½"W

171. Ink Blotter: Girl with Dog – 4½"L

172. Paper Weight: Girl with Dog – 4½"L

Row 4: **173.** Ink Well: Ring Around Rosey – 4"H

174. Pen and Pencil Tray: Ring Around Rosey and Girl with Dog – 9"L

175. Match Holder: Striker Around Top, Sand Babies – 2¼"H

176. Ink Well with Insert and Lid: Sand Babies – 4"L

PAGE 43

Row 1: **177.** Hat Pin Holder: Children (3) under Umbrella, Round Saucer Base – 4½"H

178. Hat Pin Holder: Floral, Square Saucer Base – 4½"H

179. Hat Pin Holder: The Sportsman (Aiming Gun) with Dog, Square Saucer Base – 4½"H

180. Hat Pin Holder: Floral, Square Saucer Base – 4½"H

181. Hat Pin Holder: Swans on Lake, Round Saucer Base – 4½"H

Row 2: **182.** Hat Pin Holder: Goose Girl, Square Saucer Base – 4½"H

183. Hat Pin Holder: Roses, Yellow, Square Saucer Base – 5"H

184. Hat Pin Holder: Old Ivory, Floral, Knob Handles, Round Saucer Base – 4¼"H

185. Hat Pin Holder: The Hunt (Horseman with Dogs), Reticulated Base – 4½"H

186. Hat Pin Holder: Muff Lady, Square Saucer Base – 4½"H

Row 3: **187.** Hat Pin Holder: Trees/Boy with Turkey, Round Saucer Base – 4¾"H

188. Hat Pin Holder: Roses, Pale White, Reticulated Base – 4½"H

189. Hat Pin Holder: Roses, Yellow and White, Hexagon Saucer Base – 4½"H

190. Hat Pin Holder: Peacock, Reticulated Base – 4½"H

191. Hat Pin Holder: Horsewomen with Dogs, Round Saucer Base – 4½"H

Note: Reticulated=veined or open design, hexagon=nine sides

PAGE 44

Row 1: **192.** Hat Pin Holder: Portrait Lady (with Large Purple Hat), Tapestry or Linen Finish, Reticulated Base – 4½"H

193. Hat Pin Holder: The Bathers (Castle in Background), Reticulated Base – 4½"H

194. Hat Pin Holder: Lady with Horse, Reticulated Base – 4¼"H

195. Hat Pin Holder: Stag in Stream and Gazebo, Reticulated Base, – 4½"H

196. Hat Pin Holder: Portrait Lady (with Large White Hat), Reticulated Base – 4½"H

Row 2: **197.** Hat Pin Holder: Roses, Pink, Yellow, & White, Reticulated Base – 4½"H

198. Hat Pin Holder: Roses, Pink, Reticulated Base – 4½"H

199. Hat Pin Holder: Cows, Black, Reticulated Base – 4½"H

200. Hat Pin Holder: Roses, Pink and White, Reticulated Base – 4½"H

201. Hat Pin Holder: Small Roses, Pink and White, Reticulated Base – 4½"H

Row 3: **202.** Hat Pin Holder: Christmas Cactus, Reticulated Base – 4½"H

203. Hat Pin Holder: Double Pink Rose With Daises, Pink Reticulated Base – 4½"H

204. Hat Pin Holder: Violets, Reticulated Base – 4¾"H

205. Hat Pin Holder: Pink American Beauty Rose, Reticulated Base – 4½"H

206. Hat Pin Holder: Orange, Gold Roses, Reticulated Base – 4½"H

PAGE 45

Row 1: 207. Hat Pin Holder: Sunbonnet Babies, Fishing, Round Saucer Base – 4¾"H

208. Hat Pin Holder: Sunbonnet Babies, Washing, Round Saucer Base – 4¾"H

209. Hat Pin Holder: Sunbonnet Babies, Ironing, Round Saucer Base – 4¾"H

210. Hat Pin Holder: Sunbonnet Babies, Mending, Round Saucer Base – 4¾"H

211. Hat Pin Holder: Sunbonnet Babies, Mopping, Round Saucer Base – 4¾"H

212. Hat Pin Holder: Sunbonnet Babies, Cleaning Windows, Round Saucer Base – 4¾"H, Baking, not shown, Round/Sauce Base 4¾"H

Row 2: 213. Hat Pin Holder: Peasant Musicians, (Violin & Horn), Round Base – 4½"H

214. Hat Pin Holder: Muff Lady, Round Base – 4½"H

215. Hat Pin Holder: Floral, Knob Handles, Round Base – 4½"H

216. Hat Pin Holder: Arab on Brown Horse, Round Base – 4¾"H

217. Hat Pin Holder: Work Horses, Round Base – 4¾"H

Row 3: 218. Hat Pin Holder: Farm Scene Border, Red Base, Round Base – 4½"H

219. Hat Pin Holder: Cavalier Musicians (Mandolin) Round Base – 4½"H

220. Hat Pin Holder: Corinthian (or Classic) with Acanthus Leaf, Black, Round Base – 4½"H

221. Hat Pin Holder: Arab on White Horse, Round Base – 4¾"H

222. Hat Pin Holder: Work Horses, Round Base – 4¾"H

PAGE 46

Row 1: 223. Hat Pin Holder: Lamplighter, Figural, – 4¼"H

224. Hat Pin Holder: Poppy Figural, Red, – 4¼"H

225. Hat Pin Holder: Poppy Figural, White – 4¼"H

226. Hat Pin Holder: Poppy Figural, Pink – 4¼"H

227. Hat Pin Holder: Poppy Figural, Apricot – 4¼"H

228. Hat Pin Holder: Bellringer Figural – 4½"H

Row 2: 229. Hat Pin Holder: Oyster/Pearl Figural, Orchid/White Top – 5"H

230. Hat Pin Holder: Oyster/Pearl Figural, Gold/White Top – 5"H

231. Hat Pin Holder: Clover Figural – 4¾"H

232. Hat Pin Holder: Santa Claus Figural, Red – 4¼"H

233. Hat Pin Holder: Art Nouveau Lady Figural – 4½"H

234. Hat Pin Holder: Crocus Figural – 4½"H

235. Hat Pin Holder: Coachman Figural – 4¼"H

Row 3: 236. Hat Pin Holder: Dachshund Figural, Light Brown – 4½"H

237. Hat Pin Holder: Dachshund Figural, Dark Brown – 4½"H

238. Hat Pin Holder: Owl Figural, Gray – 3¾"H

239. Hat Pin Holder: Owl Figural, Brown – 3¾"H

240. Hat Pin Holder: Penguin Figural, Black & Yellow – 5¼"H

241. Hat Pin Holder: Penguin Figural, Red & Gray – 5¼"H

PAGE 47

Row 1: 242. Hat Pin Holder: Dresser Set, Peasant Musicians (Violin & Horn) – 4½"H

243. Dresser Tray: Dresser Set, Peasant Musicians (Violin & Horn) – 11"L x 7¾"W

244. Candlestick Holder: Dresser Set, Peasant Musicians (Violin & Horn) – 5¼"H

Row 2: 245. Powder Jar (Lid): Dresser Set, Peasant Musicians (Violin & Horn) – 3¼"H

246. Trinket (Or Pin) Box & Lid: Dresser Set, Peasant Musicians (Violin & Horn) – 3½"L x 1½"W

ROYAL BAYREUTH IN COLOR

1   2   3

4   5   6

7   8   9   10   11

12   13   14   15   16

17

18

19

20   **21**   **22**   **23**

24   **25**   **26**   **27**   **28**

29

30

31

32 **33** **34**

35 **36** **37**

38 **39** **40** **41**

42 **43** **44** **45** **46**

47   48   49   50   51

52   53   54   55

56   57   58

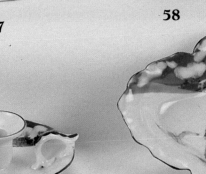

59   60   61

62   **63**   **64**   **65**

66   **67**   **68**   **69**   **70**

71   **72**   **73**   **74**   **75**   **76**

77

78   79   80   81   82

83   84   85   86   87   88

89   90   91   92

93   94   95   96

97   **98**   **99**   **100**

101   **102**   **103**

104   **105**   **106**   **107**   **108**   **109**

110   **111**   **112**   **113**   **114**

115   **116**   **117**   **118**

119   **120**   **121**   **122**   **123**   **124**

125   **126**   **127**   **128**   **129**   **130**   **131**

132   **133**   **134**   **135**   **136**   **137**   **138**

139   **140**   **141**   **142**

143   **144**   **145**   **146**   **147**

148   **149**   **150**   **151**   **152**

153   **154**   **155**   **158**   **159**

     156

     157

160   161   162

163   164   165   166   167

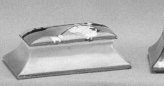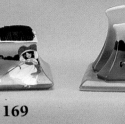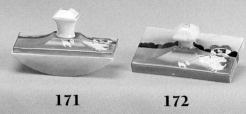

168   169   170   171   172

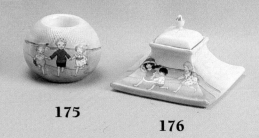

173   174   175   176

177   178   179   180   181

182   183   184   185   186

187   188   189   190   191

192   **193**   **194**   **195**   **196**

197   **198**   **199**   **200**   **201**

202   **203**   **204**   **205**   **206**

207   208   209   210   211   212

213   214   215   216   217

218   219   220   221   222

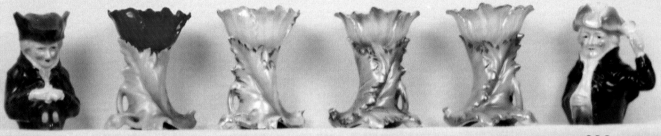

223 224 225 226 227 228

229 230 231 232 233 234 235

236 237 238 239 240 241

242

243

244

245   **246**   **247**   **248**   **249**

250   **251**   **252**

253   **254**

255

256

257

258

259

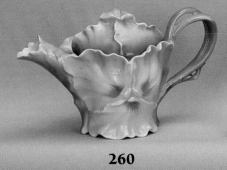

260

261

262

263

264

265

266

267

268

269

270

271   272   273   274   275

276   277   278   279   280   281   282

283   284   285   286   287   288   289

290   291   292   293   294

295   296   297   298   299   300   301   302

303   304   305   306

307

308   309   310   311

312   313   314   315

316   317   318   319   320

321   322   323   324   325   326

327   328   329   330

331   332   333   334   335   336   337

338   339   340   341   342   343

344   **345**   **346**   **347**

348

349

350

351   **352**   **353**

354   **355**

356

357

358

359

360

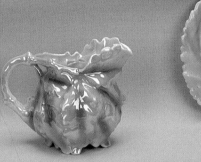

361

362

363

364

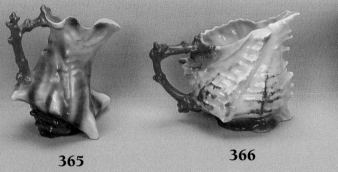

365

366

367

368

369   370   371   372   373

74   375   376   377   378   379   380   381

382   383   384   385   386

387   388   389   390   391

392   393   394   395   396   397

398

399

400

401

402

403

404

405

406

407

408

409

410

411

412

413

414

415

416

417

418

419

420

421

422   423   424   425   426   427   428

429   430   431   432   433   434   435

436   437   438   439   440   441

442   443   444   445

446   447   448

449   450   451   452

453   455

454

456

457

458

459

460

461

462

463

464

465

466

467

468

469

470

471

472

473

474   475   476

477   478   479   480   481

482   483   484   485

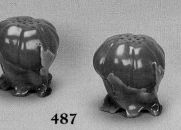

486   487   488

489 **490** **491** **492**

493 **494** **495** **496**

497 **498** **499**

500 **501**

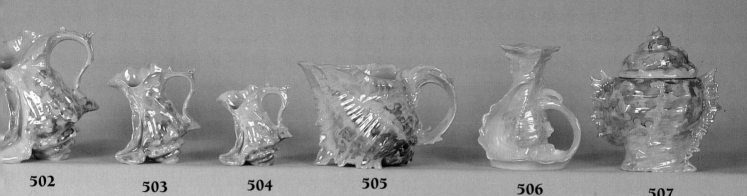

502   503   504   505   506   507

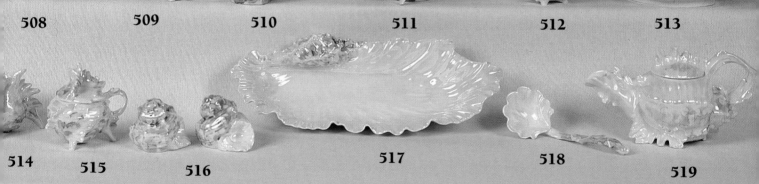

508   509   510   511   512   513

514   515   516   517   518   519

520   521   522

523   524   525

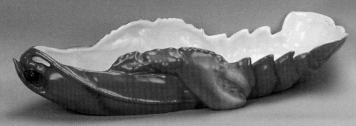

526   527   528

529   530   531   532

533   534   535   536   537

538   539   540   541   542   543

544   545   546   547   548   549   550   551

552   553   554   555   556

557   **558**   **559**   **560**

561   **562**   **563**

564   **565**   **566**

567   **568**   **569**

570　　571　　　572　　　573　　　574　　　575　　　576　　　577　　578

579　　　　580　　　　　　581　　　　　582　　　　583

584　　　585　　　　586　　　587　　　588　　　589　　　590

591 **592** **593** **594** **595**

596 **597** **598** **599** **600**

601

602

603

604

605

606

607

608

609

610

611

612

613

614

615

616

617

618

619

620

621

622

623   624   625   626   627   628   629   630

631   632   633   634   635   636

637   638   639   640   641   642   643

644   645   646   647   648   649

650　　　　　**651**　　　　　**652**　　　**653**　　　　　**654**　　　**655**

656　　　**657**　　　　　　**658**　　　　　**659**　　　　　**660**

661　　　　　　　　**663**　　　　　　**664**　　　　　**665**

　　　　662

666　　　　　　　　　　　　　　　　**668**

　　　　　　667

669   670   671   672   673

674   675   676   677

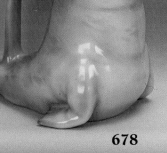

678   679   680   681

682   683   684   685

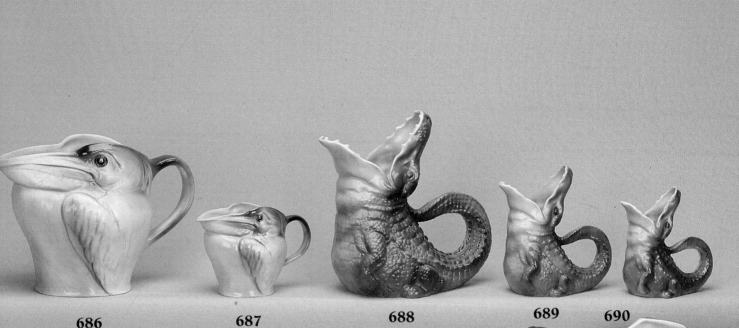

686   687   688   689   690

691   692   693   694   695

696   697   698   699

700   701   702   703

704   705   706   707   708

709   710   711

712   713   714   715

716   717   718

719

720 721 722 723

724 725 726 727 728 729

730 731 732 733 734

735 736 737

738

739

740

741

742

743

744

745

746

747

748

749

750

751

752

753

754

755

756   757   758   759

760   761   762

763   764   765   766

767   768   769   770

771   772   773   774   775   776

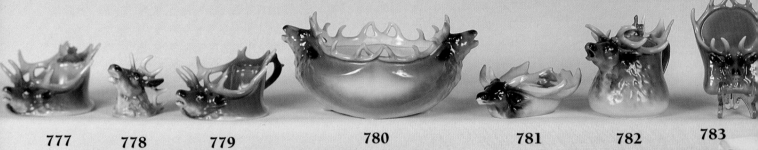

777   778   779   780   781   782   783

784   785   786   787   788   789   790   791

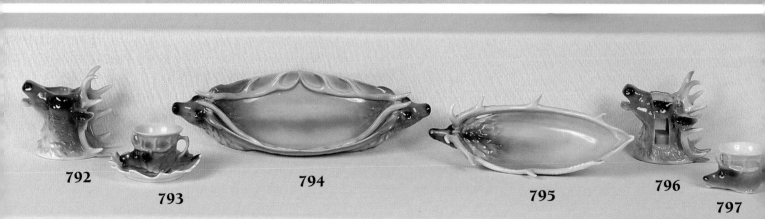

792   793   794   795   796   797

798   799   800   801   802

807   809

803   804   805   806   808   810   811   812

813   814   815   816   817

818   819   820   821   822   823   824

825   826   827   828   829   830   831

832   833   834   835   836   837   838   839   840

841   842   843   844   845   846

847   848   849

855

850 **851** **852** **853** **854**

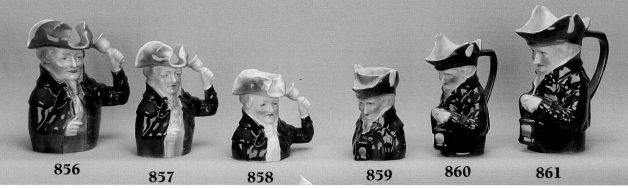

856 **857** **858** **859** **860** **861**

862 **863** **864** **865** **866** **867** **868**

869

870

871

872

873

874

875

876

877

878

879

880

881 882 883 884 885

886 887 888 889 890

891 892 893 894 895

896 897 898 899

900

901   **902**   **903**   **904**

905   **906**   **907**

908

909 910 911 912

913 914 915 916

917 918 919

920

921

922

923

924

925

926

927

928

929

930

931

932

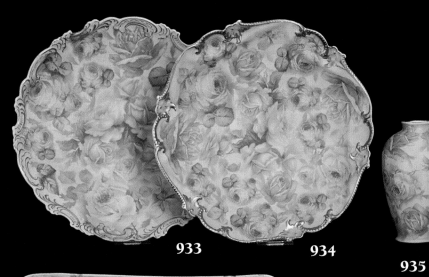

933 **934**

935 **936**

937

938

939

940

941 **942** **943** **944** **945**

946 **947** **948** **949** **950**

951

952

953

954

955

956

957

958

959

960

961

962

963

964

965

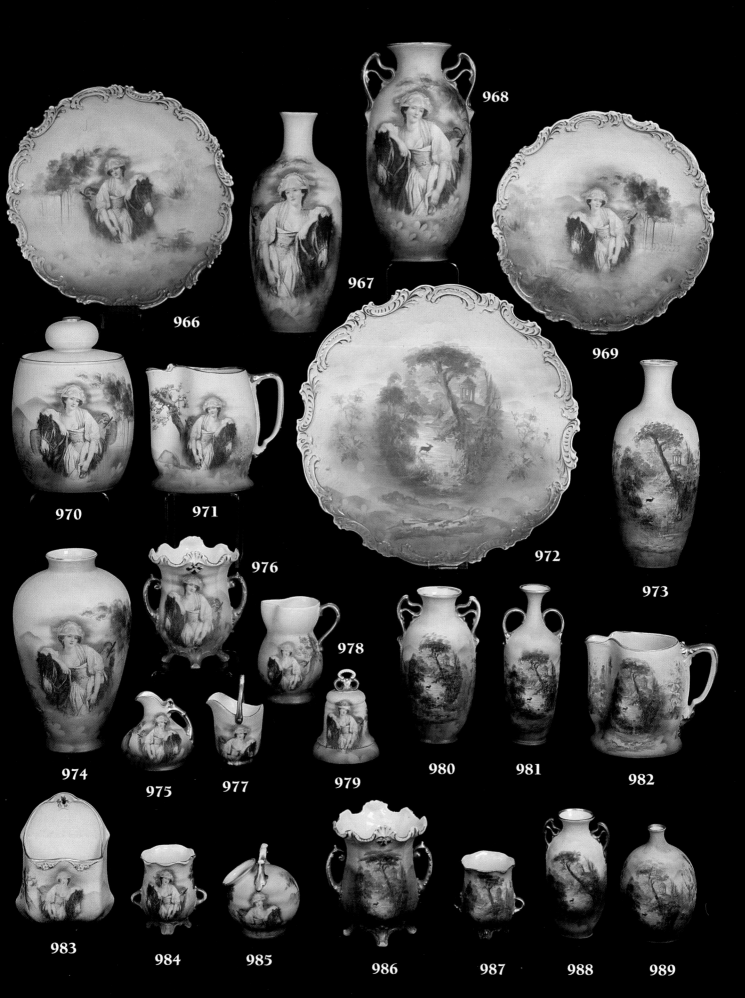

966

967

968

969

970

971

972

973

974

975

976

977

978

979

980

981

982

983

984

985

986

987

988

989

990

991

992

993

994

995

996

997

998

999

1000

1001

1002

1003

1004

1005

1006

1007

1008

1009

1010

1011

1012

1013

1014

1015

1016

1017

1018

1019

1020

1021

1022

1023

1024

1025

1026

1027

1028

1029

1030

1031

1032

1033

1034

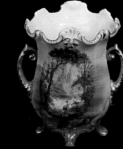

1035

1036

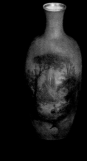

1037

1038

1039

1040

1041

1042

1043

1044

1045

1046

1047

1048

1049

1050

1051

1052

1053

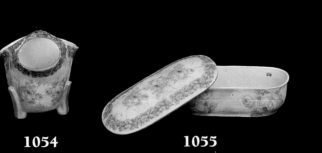

1054

1055

1056

1057

1058

1059

1060

1061

1062

1063

1064

1065

1066

1067

1068

1069

1070

1071

1072

1073

1074

1075

1076

1077

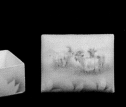

1078

1079

93

1080

1081

1082

1083

1084

1085

1086

1087

1088

1089

1090

1091

1092

1093

1094

1095

1096

1097

1098

1099

1100

1101

1102

1103

1104

1105

1106

1107

1108

1109

1110

1111

1112

1113

1114

1115

1116

1117

1118

1119

1120

1121

1122

1123

1124

1125

1126

1127

1128

1129

1131

1133

1134

1135

1136

1130

1132

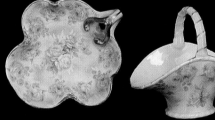

1137

1138

1139

1140

1141

1142

1143

1144

1145

1146

1147

1148

1149

1150

1151

1152

1153

1154

1155

1156

1157

1158

1159

1160

1161

1162

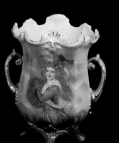

1163

1164

1165

1166

1167

1168

1169

1170

1171

1172

1173

1174

1175

1176

1177

1178

1179

1180

1181

1182

1183

1184

1185

1186

1187

1188

1189

1190   1191   1192   1193   1194

1195   1196   1197   1198   1199   1201

1200   1202

1203   1204   1205   1206   1207   1208   1209

1210   1212   1214   1216

1211   1213   1215   1217

1218

1219

1220

1221

1222

1224

1226

1228

1223

1225

1227

1229

1230

1231

1232

1234

1235

1236

1233

1237

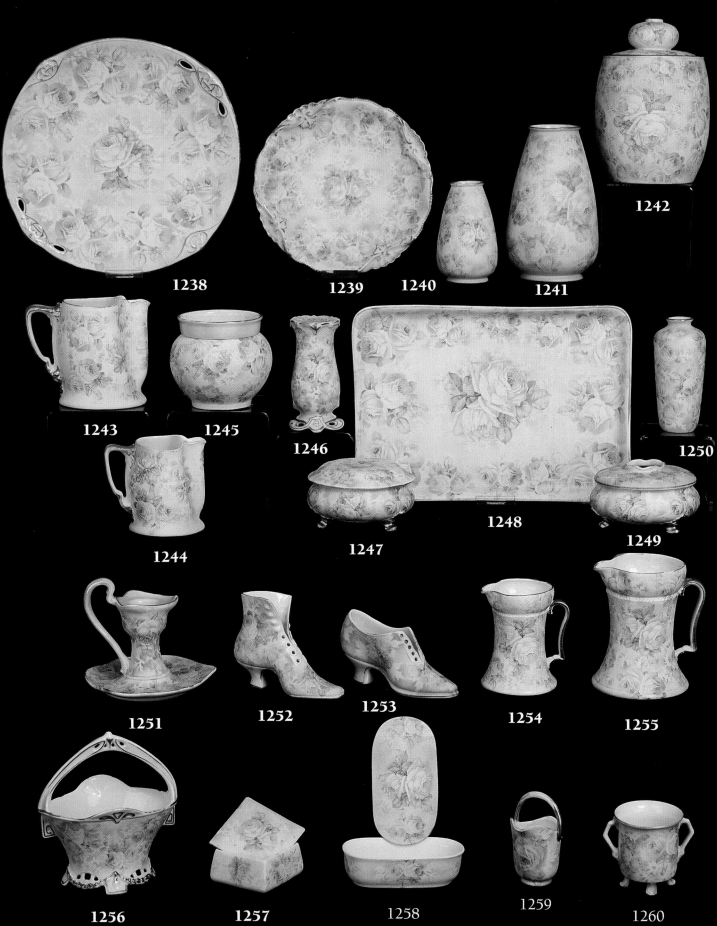

1238

1239

1240

1241

1242

1243

1245

1246

1247

1248

1249

1250

1244

1251

1252

1253

1254

1255

1256

1257

1258

1259

1260

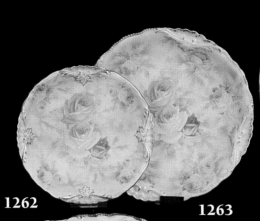

1261

1262

1263

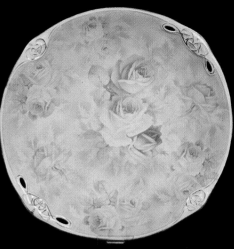

1264

1265

1266

1267

1268

1269

1270

1271

1272

1273

1274

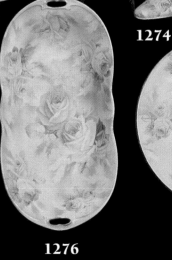

1275

1276

1277

1278

1280

1279

1281

1282

1283

1284

1285

1286

1287

1288

1289

1290

1291

1292

1293

1294

1295

1296

1297

1298

1299

1300

1301

1302

1303

1304

1305

1306

1307

1308

1309

1310

1311

1312

247. Stick Pin Holder : Dresser Set, Cavalier Musicians (Mandolin) – 2½"H
248. Trinket (or Pin) Box Lid: Dresser Set, Peasant Musicians (Violin and Horn) – 3½"L x 1½"W
249. Hair Receiver and Lid: Dresser Set, Peasant & Musicians (Violin and Horn) – 3"H

Row 3: 250. Hat Pin Holder: Dresser Set, Colonial Curtsy Scene, Reticulated Base – 4½"H
251. Dresser Tray: Dresser Set, Prince and His Lady – 11¾"L x 8 ¼"W
252. Hat Pin Holder: Dresser Set, Prince and His Lady, Reticulated Base – 4½"H
253. Hair Receiver (with Lid): Dresser Set, Colonial Curtsy Scene – 2½"H x 4½"W
254. Powder Jar (with Lid): Dresser Set, Colonial Curtsy Scene – 2½"H x 4½"W

PAGE 48
Row 1: 255. Cake Plate: Pansy, Open Handled, Pink – 10"D
256. Salt and Pepper Shaker: Pansy, Pink – 3"H
257. Mustard Pot (with Lid): Pansy, Pink – 3"H
258. Creamer: Pansy, Miniature, Purple – 4"H
259. Planter (with Liner): Pansy, Miniature, Purple – 3"H
Row 2: 260. Teapot: Pansy, Orchid – 4¾"H
261. Bowl: Pansy, Handled, Purple – 2"H x 4"L
262. Milk Pitcher: Pansy, Purple – 4½"H
263. Creamer: Pansy, Purple – 3½"H
Row 3: 264. Milk Pitcher: Chrysanthemum – 4"H
265. Creamer: Chrysanthemum – 3½"H
266. Demi-Cup Saucer: Leaf Shape for Tulip Demi-Cup – 3¾"D
267. Demi-Cup: Tulip – 1¾"H
Row 4: 268. Creamer: Geranium – 3¾"H
269. Relish Tray: Poinsettia – 7½"L x 4¼"W
270. Creamer: Iris – 4¼"H

PAGE 49
Row 1: 271. Water Pitcher: Poppy, Apricot Satin with Gold Trim – 6½"H
272. Sugar (with Lid): Poppy, Footed, White Satin with Gold Trim – 3½"H
273. Cake Plate: Poppy, White Satin with Gold Trim – 10"D
274. Creamer: Poppy, Footed (Matches Footed Sugar), White Satin with Gold Trim – 3¾"H
275. Planter (with Insert): Poppy, Orchid and White Satin – 6½"H
Row 2: 276. Nut Bowl: Poppy, Orchid and White Satin – 4¾"H
277. Hair Receiver (with Lid): Poppy, Footed, Purple and White Satin – 2¼"H
278. Bowl: Poppy, Footed, Small Size (no Lid) – 1½"H x 3½"D
279. Tea Strainer: Poppy – 5½"H
280. Salt Dip: Poppy, Yellow – 1¾"L x 1"D
281. Ladle: Poppy, White Satin – 5"L
282. Nappy: Poppy, Handled, Orchid and White Satin – 5½"D
Row 3: 283. Planter (Liner): Pansy, Miniature – 3"H
284. Salt Dip: Pansy – 1"H x 1¾"D
285. Demi-Cup: Pansy – 1¾"H & Saucer – 4"D
286. Bowl: Pansy – 6"D
287. Low, Candlestick: Pansy, Handled – 2¾"H
288. Hat Pin Holder: Crocus – 4½"H
289. Creamer: Orchid – 4½"H

PAGE 50

Row 1: **290.** Water Pitcher: Red Poppy – 6¾"H

291. Creamer: Red Poppy – 3¾"H

292. Plate: Red Poppy – 8½"D

293. Toothpick Holder: Red Poppy – 3"H

294. Cracker Jar (with Lid): Red Poppy – 7"H

Row 2: **295.** Bowl (with Lid): Red Poppy – 2½"H

296. Bowl (with Lid): Red Poppy – 3½"H

297. Nut Bowl: Red Poppy – 2½"H x 4¾"D

298. Nut Cup: Red Poppy, Footed – 1½"H x 3"D

299. Salt Dip: Red Poppy – 1"H x 1¾"D

300. Mustard Pot (with Lid): Red Poppy – 3¼"H

301. Sugar (with Lid): Red Poppy – 3¼"H x 4½"W

302. Teapot (with Lid): Red Poppy – 4½"H

Row 3: **303.** Tea Strainer: Red Poppy – 5½"L

304. Salt and Pepper Shakers: Red Poppy – 2¾"H

305. Ladle: Red Poppy – 5"L

306. Sugar (with Lid): Red Tomato, Footed – 3¾"H

307. Teapot (with Lid): Red Tomato, Footed – 4¼"H

PAGE 51

Row 1: **308.** Open Compote: Red Poppy – 3½"

309. Plate: Red Poppy – 8¼"D

310. Milk Pitcher: Red Poppy – 4½"H

311. Hat Pin Holder: Red Poppy, Footed – 4"H

Row 2: **312.** Bowl: Poppy, Footed, Yellow and White Satin Finish – 3"H x 5½"D

313. Bowl: Red Poppy, Footed – 2¾"H

314. Candlestick: Red Poppy – 5"W

315. Hanging Wall Pocket or Wall Vase: Red Poppy – 9"L x 5¾"W

Row 3: **316.** Creamer: Poppy, Yellow/White Satin Finish – 3¾"H

317. Creamer: Red Poppy – 3¾"H

318. Plate: Poppy, Yellow/White Finish – 6"D

319. Creamer: Poppy, Footed, White Satin Finish – 3¾"H

320. Open Sugar: Poppy, Footed, White Satin Finish – 2¼"H

Row 4: **321.** Nappy: Poppy, Handled, Orchid/White Satin Finish – 5¼"L

322. Nappy: Poppy, Handled, Yellow/White Satin Finish – 5"L x 1½"H

323. Nut Dish: Red Poppy, Footed, Small Size – 1½"H

324. Salt Dip: Poppy, Footed, Yellow – 1½"W x ¾"H

325. Cup: Red Poppy, Footed – 3½"W

326. Chocolate Cup: Poppy, Footed, Yellow – 3"H

PAGE 52

Row 1: **327.** Plate: Lemon – 6"D

328. Sugar (with Lid): Pineapple – 5"H

329. Sugar (with Lid): Orange, Footed – 4½"H

330. Plate: Corn – 8½"D

Row 2: **331.** Mustard Pot (with Lid) and Spoon: Red Pepper – 3½"H

332. Demi-Cup: Lemon – 2"H and Saucer – 4"D
333. Salt and Pepper Shakers: Orange, Footed – 2½"H
334. Condiment Set with Spoon: Fig – 4"H
335. Salt Shaker: Cucumber – 4"H
336. Salt and Pepper Shakers: Corn – 2¾"H
337. Salt and Pepper Shakers: Apple – 2¼"H

Row 3: 338. Wall Pocket or Vase: Peach – 9"L
339. Salt Dip: Radish – 1½"H
340. Salt Shaker: Pine Cone – 3½"H
341. Nut Bowl: Almond, Footed – 5"H
342. Nut Dish: Almond – 3½"H
343. Wall Pocket or Vase: Strawberry – 9"L

PAGE 53
Row 1: 344. Plate: Lettuce Leaf – 7"D
345. Plate: Lettuce Leaf – 6"D
346. Plate: Lettuce Leaf – 4"D
347. Plate: Lettuce Leaf – 4"D, Lettuce Leaf is used for Underplates for the Tomato Pieces also.

Row 2: 348. Plate: Leaf and Flower, Handled – 6"D
349. Nut Bowl: Almond, Footed – 5"W x 2"H
350. Plate: Leaf and Flower, Handled – 7"D

Row 3: 351. Creamer: Sun Flower – 3¾"H
352. Milk Pitcher: Sun Flower – 4½"H
353. Bowl with Lid: Rose, Covered – 3¾"W x 1¾"H

Row 4: 354. Saucer: Rose – 5"D
355. Cup: Rose – 2"H
356. Bowl: Rose, Footed – 5"W x 2¾"H

PAGE 54
Row 1: 357. Oak Leaf Berry Set: Large Bowl – 9"D, Dessert – 5½"D
Row 2: 358. Milk Pitcher: Oak Leaf, Green with Red Handle – 4½"H
359. Water Pitcher: Maple Leaf, Red, Green, and Yellow – 6½"H
360. Milk Pitcher: Oak Leaf, White Satin – 4½"H

Row 3: 361. Creamer: Maple Leaf, Yellow and Green – 3¼"H
362. Creamer: Oak Leaf, Green – 3¾"H
363. Plate: Oak Leaf, Green – 6"D
364. Salt Shaker: Oak Leaf, Green – 3"H

Row 4: 365. Creamer: Boot Shape Shell, Twig or Coral Handle – 3¾"H
366. Creamer: Spiky Shell – 3¾"H
367. Milk Pitcher: Boot Shape Shell, Twig or Coral Handle – 4"H

PAGE 55
Row 1: 368. Oak Leaf Chocolate Set: White Satin with Gold Trim, Footed: Chocolate Pot with Lid – 8"H, Cup – 3"H, Saucer – 4½"D
Row 2: 369. Bowl: Oak Leaf, Footed, White Satin with Gold Trim – 9"L x 6½"W
370. Nappy: Oak Leaf, Handled, Green Satin – 7½"L x 6"W
371. Creamer: Oak Leaf, Green Satin – 4"H

372. Open Sugar: Oak Leaf, Green Satin – 3"H

373. Celery: Oak Leaf, White Satin with Gold Trim – 12¾"L x 5½"W

Row 3: **374.** Salt Shaker: Spiky Shell, White Satin – 3¼"H

375. Ashtray: Nautilus Shell, White Satin – 5"L x 4"W

376. Demi-cup: Spiky Shell, White Satin, – 1¾"H Saucer: Spiky Shell, White Satin – 4"D

377. Open Sugar: Nautilus Shell, Multi-Color – 2½"H

378. Creamer: Nautilus Shell, Multi-Color – 2¼"H

379. Wall Match Holder: Spiky Shell, White Satin – 5"L

380. Relish: Nautilus Shell, White Satin – (Unusual Black Decoration on Shell and also seen on a Water Pitcher) – 8"L x 5"W

381. Nut or Mint Dish: Spiky Shell, White Satin – 2¼"H

PAGE 56

Row 1: **382.** Hanging Match Holder: Oyster and Pearl – 4½"L

383. Ashtray: Oyster and Pearl – 4"L

384. Tray: Oyster and Pearl – 9¾"L x 7"W

385. Sugar with Lid: Oyster and Pearl – 1¾"H

386. Creamer: Oyster and Pearl – 2¼"H

Row 2: **387.** Nut Bowl Set: Poppy, Peach Satin Finish, Master Bowl: Footed – 3"H x 4¾"W, Small Matching Nut Bowls: (6) Footed – 1½"H x 3"W

388. Basket: Open Lattice, Red – 4"H

389. Creamer: Open Lattice, Red – 3"H

390. Bowl or Ashtray: Open Lattice, (Heart Shape) - Red – 4¾"W

391. Cup: Open Lattice – 3¼"H, Saucer: – Red – 4¼"W

Row 3: **392.** Demi-Cup: Lobster – 1¾"H, Saucer: – 4¼"W

393. Match Holder: Clown, White Satin – 3"H

394. Creamer: Clown, (Rare) Green – 3½"H

395. Candy Dish: Clown, Red – 7"L x 6"W

396. Ashtray: Red Devil Head – 5"H

397. Hanging Match Holder: Devil/Cards, Full Figure – 6"L

PAGE 57

Row 1: **398.** Bowl: Strawberry with Blossom – 9½"W

399. Cracker Jar (with Lid): Strawberry – 6½"H

400. Water Pitcher: Shell (with Coral or Twig Handle), Boot Shape – 8"H x 7½"W

401. Chocolate Pot: Poppy, Yellow Satin, – 8¾"H; Cup: Poppy, Yellow Satin – 3"H

Row 2: **402.** Bowl: Radish – 2½"H

403. Wall Vase: Apple – 9"L

404. Creamer: Grape, Purple – 4"H

405. Sugar (with Lid): Grape, Purple – 3¾"H

406. Toothpick Holder: Red Pepper – 1¾"H

407. Bowl: Almond, Footed – 2¼"H x 5"W

408. Milk Pitcher: Iris – 5"H

Row 3: **409.** Tea Strainer: Pansy – 5½"L

410. Tea Strainer: Sun Flower – 5½"L

411. Poppy Mayonnaise Set: White Satin, Bowl: – 5¼"D, Underplate – 6"D

412. Relish: Oak Leaf, White Satin and Gold – 7¼"L x 4½"W

413. Sugar with Lid: Rose, Yellow – 2¼"H

414. Candlestick: Rose, Handled, Red – 2¾"H

Row 4: **415.** Creamer: Seal (Ad piece – Old Ben, Catalina Island, CA.) – 4¾"H

416. Creamer: Calico Cat – 4¾"H

417. Creamer: Penguin, Black and White – 4¾"H

418. Creamer: Pig, Red – 4¼"H

419. Creamer: Flounder, Yellow – 4¼"H

420. Humidor (with Lid): Horse Head, White with Gold Trim – 5¾"H

421. Milk Pitcher: Horse Head, White with Gold Trim – 5"H

PAGE 58

Row 1: **422.** Water Pitcher: Sun Flower – 6½"H

423. Water Pitcher: Geranium – 6½"H

424. Salt and Pepper Shakers: Geranium – 2¾"H

425. Demi-Cup: Pear – 1¾"H x 3¼"L, Saucer: – 4"W

426. Water Pitcher: Pear – 7½"H

427. Milk Pitcher: Pear – 5½"H

428. Creamer: Pear – 4½"H

Row 2: **429.** Mustard Pot (with Lid): Rose – 3"H

430. Cup: Rose – 1¾"H, Saucer: – 4½"D

431. Salt and Pepper Shakers: Rose – 2¼"H

432. Toothpick Holder: Rose – 2¼"H

433. Cup: Flower – 2"H, Saucer: – 4"W

434. Salt Dip: Clover – 1¾"D x 1"H

435. Saucer or Underplate: Flower – 4¼"D

Row 3: **436.** Milk Pitcher: Rose – 4½"H

437. Candlestick Holder: Rose – 2¾"H x 7"L

438. Bowl: Rose, Footed, Large Size – 5"H x 8"W

439. Sugar (with Lid): Rose – 2½"H

440. Creamer: Rose – 3"H

441. Bowl: Rose, Footed – 3"H x 5"W

PAGE 59

Row 1: **442.** Creamer: Apple – 3¾"H

443. Water Pitcher: Apple – 6"H

444. Milk Pitcher: Apple – 4"H

445. Lemonade Pitcher: Apple – 7"H

Row 2: **446.** Milk Pitcher: Watermelon – 5"H

447. Water Pitcher: Watermelon – 6½"H

448. Creamer: Watermelon – 4"H

Row 3: **449.** Bowl: Apple with Lid: Large Size – 3½"H

450. Bowl: Apple with Lid: Small Size – 3"H

451. Teapot with Lid: Apple, Small Size – 3¾"H

452. Bowl: Apple with Lid, Medium Size – 4"H

Row 4: **453.** Mustard Pot with Lid: Apple – 3½"H

454. Demi-Cup and Saucer: Apple – 1¾"H

455. Plate: Leaf Shape – 4½"D

PAGE 60

Row 1: 456. Marmalade with Lid: Orange, Large Size – 6"H

457. Water Pitcher: Orange – 7"H

458. Milk Pitcher: Orange – 5"H

459. Creamer with Lid: Orange – 4½"H

Row 2: 460. Creamer: Orange – 4"H

461. Mustard Pot with Lid: Orange, Footed – 3½"H

462. Sugar with Lid: Orange, Footed – 4"H

463. Demi-Cup: Orange – 2"H; Saucer: Orange – 4¾"D

464. Mustard Pot (with Lid): Tomato, Footed – 3½"H

Row 3: 465. Plate: Tomato Vine with Blossoms – 7"D

466. Creamer: Tomato – 4½"H

467. Bowl: Tomato – 4½"D

468. Bowl: Radish, Footed – 5"D

Row 4: 469. Salt and Pepper Shaker: Red Chili Pepper – 4"H

470. Salt Shaker: Radish – 3"H

471. Salt Shaker: Red Pepper – 2¾"H

472. Teapot with Lid: Tomato, Large Size – 4¼"H

473. Plate: Lettuce Leaf, Oval Shape – 5¼"L x 4½"W

PAGE 61

Row 1: 474. Water Pitcher: Tomato – 6"H

475. Cracker Jar with Lid: Tomato – 6¼"H

476. Plate: Tomato Vine – 9"D

Row 2: 477. Bowl: Tomato Leaf with Blossoms – 5½"D

478. Bowl with Lid: Tomato, Small Size – 2½"H

479. Bowl with Lid: Tomato, Large Size – 3¾"H

480. Bowl with Lid: Tomato, Medium Size – 2¾"H

481. Milk Pitcher: Tomato – 4½"H

Row 3: 482. Teapot with Lid: Tomato, Small Size – 5"W x 3¾"H

483. Demi-Cup: Tomato – 2"H

484. Underplate: Tomato Vine – 5¼"D

485. Sugar with Lid: Tomato – 3½"H

Row 4: 486. Creamer: Tomato – 3"H

487. Salt and Pepper Shakers: Tomato, Footed – 2½"H

488. Gravy Boat (with Underplate: row 3 #3) – 2½"H

PAGE 62

Row 1: 489. Creamer: Lemon – 3¾"H

490. Lemonade Pitcher: Lemon – 7½"H

491. Milk Pitcher: Lemon – 4¾"H

492. Water Pitcher: Lemon – 6½"H

Row 2: 493. Plate: Lettuce Leaf with Blossoms – 5¼"D

494. Mustard Pot with Lid: Lemon – 3½"H

495. Sugar with Lid: Lemon – 3½"H

496. Teapot with Lid: Lemon – 4¼"H

Row 3: 497. Milk Pitcher: Grape, Yellow/White Satin Finish – 4½"H

498. Water Pitcher: Grape, Yellow/White Satin Finish – 6"H

499. Teapot with Lid: Grape, White Satin – 4¾"H

Row 4: **500.** Sugar with Lid: Grape, Yellow/White Satin Finish – 3½"H

501. Teapot with Lid: Grape, Yellow/White Satin Finish – 4¾"H

PAGE 63

Row 1: **502.** Water Pitcher: Spiky Shell, Boot Shape, White Satin Finish – 7"H

503. Milk Pitcher: Spiky Shell, Boot Shape, White Satin Finish – 5½"H

504. Creamer: Spiky Shell, Boot Shape, White Satin Finish – 4¾"H

505. Water Pitcher: Spiky Shell, White Satin Finish, Bulbous – 5½"H

506. Candlestick Holder: Spiky Shell, White Satin Finish, Tall Size – 6¾"H

507. Cracker Jar with Lid: Spiky Shell, White Satin Finish – 8"H

Row 2: **508.** Sugar with Lid: Spiky Shell, White Satin Finish – 4"H

509. Salt and Pepper Shakers: Spiky Shell, White Satin Finish – 3"H

510. Creamer: Spiky Shell, White Satin Finish – 4¼"H

511. Bowl: Spiky Shell, White Satin Finish, Large Size – 8"W x 4½"H

512. Mustard Pot with Lid: Spiky Shell, White Satin Finish, Footed – 3½"H

513. Gravy Boat: Spiky Shell, White Satin Finish – 2½"H; Underplate, Handled: Spiky Shell – 7"L x 5½"W

Row 3: **514.** Toothpick Holder: Spiky Shell, White Satin Finish, Footed – 3"H

515. Mustard Pot with Lid: Spiky Shell, White Satin Finish – 3½"H

516. Salt and Pepper Shakers: Nautilus Shell, White Satin Finish – 2¼"H

517. Celery: Nautilus Shell, White Satin Finish – 12¾"L x 5"W

518. Ladle: Spiky Shell, White Satin Finish – 5½"H

519. Teapot with Lid: Spiky Shell, White Satin Finish – 4½"H

PAGE 64

Row 1: **520.** Water Pitcher: Red Lobster – 6¾"H

521. Milk Pitcher: Red Lobster – 4½"H

522. Humidor with Lid: Red Lobster – 7½"H

Row 2: **523.** Creamer: Red Lobster – 3¾"H

524. Bowl: Red Lobster, Large Size – 3¾"W x 8"L

525. Sugar with Lid: Red Lobster, Large Size – 4¾"H

Row 3: **526.** Celery Bowl: Red Lobster – 12"L x 4½"W

527. Sugar with Lid: Red Lobster, Small Size – 4"H

528. Creamer: Red Lobster – 3¾"H

Row 4: **529.** Mustard Pot with Lid and Spoon: Red Lobster – 4"H

530. Candy Dish: Red Lobster – 3"H

531. Cup: Red Lobster – 1¾"H

532. Salt and Pepper Shakers: Red Lobster – 3"H

PAGE 65

Row 1: **533.** Water Pitcher: Strawberry – 6¾"H

534. Salt Shaker: Cherry – 3"H

535. Milk Pitcher: Strawberry – 4¾"H

536. Cracker Jar with Lid: Strawberry – 6"H

537. Plate: Strawberry Leaf – 7"D

Row 2: **538.** Cracker Jar with Lid: Pineapple – 6¾"H

539. Creamer: Strawberry – 4"H

540. Sugar with Lid: Strawberry – 3¾"H

541. Mustard Pot with Spoon: Strawberry – 3¾"H

542. Salt and Pepper Shakers: Strawberry – 2"H

543. Marmalade: Pineapple – 5"H, Underplate; Pineapple – 6"D

Row 3:
544. Demi-Cup: Lobster and Leaves, Red, Cup – 2"H; Saucer – 4¼"D

545. Dish: Lobster, Red – 6¾"L x 3½"H

546. Salt Dip: Lobster, Red – 2¾"W

547. Mustard Pot with Lid and Spoon: Lobster, Red – 4½"H

548. Water Pitcher: Lobster, Purple Satin Finish – 6¾"H

549. Creamer: Lobster, Purple Satin Finish – 6¾"H

550. Salt and Pepper Shakers: Lobster, Red – 3"H

551. Ashtray: Lobster Claw, Red – 6¼"L

Row 4:
552. Shell Dish: Chick Perched on Shell, and Cock-fight in Bottom – 4½"L x 2"H

553. Milk Pitcher: Chamois – 5½"H

554. Creamer: Chamois – 5¼"H

555. Open Sugar: Crow, Black – 3¾"W x 5½"L x 2"H

556. Open Sugar: Eagle – 2"H

PAGE 66

Row 1:
557. Portrait Bowl: Muff Lady and Lady with Horse (in Medallions), Satin Finish – 10½"D

558. Bowl: Art Nouveau Lady – 3"H x 5¾"W

559. Creamer: Rabbit – 4"H

560. Milk Pitcher: Bear – 5"H

Row 2:
561. Salt and Pepper Shakers: Horse Head – 3¼"H

562. Creamer: Rose Tapestry, Black (Only One Reported in this Color) – 3"H

563. Salt and Pepper Shakers: Poppy, Peach Satin Finish – 2¾"H

Row 3:
564. Salt and Pepper Shakers: Plum – 2¾"H

565. Salt and Pepper Shakers: Lemon – 3"H

566. Salt and Pepper Shakers: Corn – 3"H

Row 4:
567. Salt and Pepper Shakers: Alligator – 3¼"

568. Salt and Pepper Shakers: Clown, Red, Green and Yellow – 3½"H

569. Salt and Pepper Shakers: Standing Trout – 3½"H

PAGE 67

Row 1:
570. Hat Pin Holder: Penguin – 5½"H

571. Water Pitcher: Penguin, Red, Gray, Yellow, (Also Seen in Black and White) – 7¾"H

572. Milk Pitcher: Girl with Pitcher – 5"H

573. Ashtray: Devil Head – 2½"H x 5"L

574. Demi-Cup: Red Devil – 2¾"H

575. Stamp Box with Lid: Devil and Cards, Divided Section Inside – 2¼'H x 3¾"L

576. Open Sugar: Devil and Cards – 2¾"H

577. Ashtray: Devil and Cards, with Attached Match Holder – 3¾"H x 4"L

578. Ladies Purse or Bag: Drawstring, Green – 10"H

Row 2:
579. Water Pitcher: Grape, White Satin Finish – 6¼"H

580. Milk Pitcher: Grape, White Satin Finish – 4¼"H

581. Bowl: Grape, White Satin Finish – 6"H x 9½"L

582. Mustard Pot with Lid: Grape, White Satin Finish – 3¼"H

583. Cracker Jar with Lid: Grape, White Satin Finish – 7¼"H

Row 3: 584. Salt and Pepper Shakers: Grape, White Satin Finish – 3"H

585. Wall Pocket or Vase: Grape, White Satin Finish – 9"H

586. Marmalade Jar with Lid: Grape, (Underplate Reported) – 4"H

587. Demi-Cup: Grape, White Satin Finish – 2"H

588. Sugar with Lid: Grape, White Satin Finish – 3½"H

589. Creamer: Grape, White Satin Finish – 3¾"H

590. Teapot with Lid: Grape, White Satin Finish – 4¾"H

PAGE 68
Row 1: 591. Water Pitcher: Mouse, Gray – 7½"H

592. Milk Pitcher: Mouse, Gray – 5"H

593. Creamer: Mouse, Gray – 4½"H

594. Creamer: Mouse, Brown – 4½"H

595. Water Pitcher: Rabbit (Rare) – 7½"H

Row 2: 596. Water Pitcher: Duck – 6¾"H

597. Milk Pitcher: Duck – 4½"H

598. Creamer: Duck – 3¾"H

599. Milk Pitcher: Shell with Seahorse Handle – 4¾"H

600. Water Pitcher: Shell with Seahorse Handle – 7½"H

Row 3: 601. Water Pitcher: Oak Leaf, White Satin with Gold Trim – 6½"H

602. Milk Pitcher: Oak Leaf, White Satin with Gold Trim – 4¾"H

603. Water Pitcher: Poppy, White Satin with Gold Trim – 6¼"H

Row 4: 604. Poppy Chocolate Set: White Satin with Gold Trim Chocolate Pot – 8½"H; Cups – 2¾"H; Saucers – 4¼"D

PAGE 69
Row 1: 605. Water Pitcher: Rooster, Multi-Color – 7¼"H

606. Creamer: Rooster, Multi-Color – 4¼"H

607. Creamer: Rooster, Black and Red – 4¼"H

608. Creamer: Rooster, Black and Gray – 4¼"H

609. Water Pitcher: Rooster, Black and Gray – 7¼"H

Row 2: 610. Creamer: Bird of Paradise, (Ad Piece, Newport) – 3¾"H

611. Milk Pitcher: Robin – 7"H

612. Water Pitcher: Robin – 6¾"H

613. Creamer: Robin – 3¾"H

614. Ashtray: Robin – 3"H x 4"W

Row 3: 615. Milk Pitcher: Parakeet – 4½"H

616. Creamer: Parakeet – 3½"H

617. Water Pitcher: Parakeet – 6¼"H

618. Creamer: Parakeet, Aqua and Yellow – 3¾"H

Row 4: 619. Milk Pitcher: Cockatoo, White and Yellow – 4¾"H

620. Wall String Holder: Rooster, Multi-Color, – 3"W x 6"L

621. Milk Pitcher: Rooster, White – 5"H

622. Open Sugar: Rooster – 3"H x 5½"L

PAGE 70
Row 1: 623. Water Pitcher: Squirrel (Rare) – 8"H

624. Milk Pitcher: Squirrel – 5½"H

625. Creamer: Squirrel – 4¾"H
626. Water Pitcher: Monkey – 6½"H
627. Milk Pitcher: Monkey – 5"H
628. Creamer: Monkey – 4"H
629. Water Pitcher: Chick – 7"H
630. Creamer: Chick – 4"H

Row 2: **631.** Milk Pitcher: Butterfly, (Closed Wing) – 4¼"H
632. Water Pitcher: Butterfly (Closed Wing) – 6½"H
633. Creamer: Butterfly (Closed Wing) – 3½"H
634. Water Pitcher: Fish Head – 6"H
635. Lemonade Pitcher: Fish Head – 7½"H
636. Creamer: Fish Head – 4"H

Row 3: **637.** Creamer: Cockatoo – 4"H
638. Creamer: Tiger, (Rare) – 4"H
639. Creamer: Leopard, (Rare) – 3"H
640. Ashtray: Turkey – 5"L x 4"H
641. Pipe Rest: Basset Hound – 5½"L x 3"H
642. Milk Pitcher: Gorilla – 5¼"H
643. Milk Pitcher: Bear – 5¼"H

Row 4: **644.** Ashtray: Eagle – 5"L
645. Ashtray: Swan (or Mallard) – 2½"H x 6"W
646. Ashtray: Robin – 5"L
647. Hat Pin Holder: Santa Claus, Green – 4"H
648. Bowl: Perch – 2¾"H x 6"L
649. Box (with Lid): Boar – 5½"L

PAGE 71
Row 1: **650.** Water Pitcher: Saint Bernard – 5"H
651. Milk Pitcher: Saint Bernard – 3¾"H
652. Creamer: Saint Bernard – 3"H
653. Milk Pitcher: Black Cat – 5½"H
654. Creamer: Gray Cat – 4¾"H
655. Creamer: Black Cat – 4¾"H

Row 2: **656.** Candlestick Holder: Basset Hound – 4"H
657. Humidor with Lid: Basset Hound – 5½"H
658. Milk Pitcher: Dachshund – 5"H
659. Water Pitcher: Dachshund – 6"H
660. Creamer: Dachshund – 4"H

Row 3: **661.** Milk Pitcher: Poodle, Black – 5¼"H
662. Creamer: Poodle, Black and White – 4½"H
663. Creamer: Poodle, Gray, – 4½"H
664. Creamer: Poodle, Black, – 4½"H
665. Creamer: Bear, Brown and Gray – 4¼"H

Row 4: **666.** Creamer: Chimpanzee – 4"H
667. Humidor with Lid: Gorilla, Gray and Black – 6½"H
668. Hanging Match Holder: Chimpanzee – 2¼"W x 5"L

PAGE 72

Row 1: **669.** Water Pitcher: Perch – 7¼"H

670. Creamer: Perch – 4"H

671. Water Pitcher: Standing Trout – 8"H

672. Milk Pitcher: Standing Trout – 6¼"H

673. Creamer: Standing Trout – 4½"H

Row 2: **674.** Creamer: Fish Head – 4"H

675. Milk Pitcher: Fish Head – 5"H

676. Water Pitcher: Fish Head – 6"H

677. Lemonade Pitcher: Fish Head – 7½"H

Row 3: **678.** Water Pitcher: Seal, Gray – 6¾"H

679. Milk Pitcher: Seal, Brown – 4¾"H

680. Creamer: Seal, Gray – 4"H

681. Creamer: Flounder – 4"H

Row 4: **682.** Milk Pitcher: Shell, Lobster Handle – 3"H

683. Creamer: Shell, Lobster Handle – 2½"H

684. Sugar with Lid: Shell, Lobster Handle, Mint Green and White – 3"H

685. Water Pitcher: Shell, Lobster Handle – 4"H x 8½"L

PAGE 73

Row 1: **686.** Water Pitcher: Pelican – 6"H

687. Creamer: Pelican – 3½"H

688. Water Pitcher: Alligator – 7"H

689. Milk Pitcher: Alligator – 5"H

690. Creamer: Alligator – 4½"H

Row 2: **691.** Creamer: Eagle – 3½"H

692. Ashtray: Eagle – 4½"L x 4"W

693. Candlestick Holder: Eagle – 4"H

694. Milk Pitcher: Eagle – 4¼"H

695. Water Pitcher: Eagle – 6"H

Row 3: **696.** Water Pitcher: Frog, Red – 4¾"H

697. Milk Pitcher: Frog, Green – 3"H

698. Milk Pitcher: Frog, Red – 3"H

699. Creamer: Frog, Green – 2½"H

Row 4: **700.** Candlestick Holder: Owl – 5"L x 3¾"H

701. Creamer: Owl – 3¾"H

702. Hat Pin Holder: Owl – 3¾"H

703. Milk Pitcher: Owl – 4¾"H

PAGE 74

Row 1: **704.** Water Pitcher: Beetle – 6"H

705. Creamer: Lady Bug (Cut-Out Under Eyes) – 3¾"H

706. Creamer: Lady Bug (Solid Under Eyes) – 3¾"H

707. Milk Pitcher: Lady Bug (Cut-Out Under Eyes) – 4¾"H

708. Water Pitcher: Lady Bug (Cut-Out Under Eyes) – 6"H

Row 2: **709.** Water Pitcher: Snake – 6¼"H

710. Milk Pitcher: Snake – 4¾"H

711. Creamer: Snake – 3¾"H

Row 3:   **712.** Creamer: Turtle – 2"H

          713. Milk Pitcher: Turtle – 2½"H

          714. Water Pitcher: Turtle – 3¼"H

          715. Lemonade Pitcher: Turtle – 4½"H

Row 4:   **716.** Sugar with Lid: Turtle – 2¾"W x 5"L

          717. Hanging Match Holder: Ibex – 4½"H

          718. Milk Pitcher: Turtle, Gold Overlay on Shell – 2½"H

PAGE 75

Row 1:   **719.** Creamer: Bull, Black – 3½"H

          720. Milk Pitcher: Butterfly (Open-Wing) – 4"H

          721. Water Pitcher: Butterfly (Open-Wing) – 6½"H

          722. Creamer: Butterfly, (Open-Wing) – 3¼"H

          723. Creamer: Cow, Black – 4"H

Row 2:   **724.** Creamer: Cow, Red – 4"H

          725. Milk Pitcher: Water Buffalo, Gray – 4¼"H

          726. Creamer: Water Buffalo, Gray – 3¾"H

          727. Milk Pitcher: Water Buffalo, Black – 4¼"H

          728. Creamer: Water Buffalo, Black – 3¾"H

          729. Creamer: Bull, Brown and White – 3½"H

Row 3:   **730.** Milk Pitcher: Crow, Black – 5½"H

          731. Creamer: Crow, Black and White – 4¾"H

          732. Creamer: Crow, Black – 4¾"H

          733. Creamer: Bull, Black and White – 3½"H

          734. Creamer: Bull, Gray – 3½"H

Row 4:   **735.** Creamer: Mountain Goat – 3½"H

          736. Ashtray: Mountain Goat – 5½"L x 4"W

          737. Hanging Match Holder: Mountain Goat – 4½"L x 3"W

PAGE 76

Row 1:   **738.** Creamer: Art Nouveau Lady – 3½"H

          739. Water Pitcher: Art Nouveau Lady – 6"H

          740. Candlestick Holder, Short: Art Nouveau Lady – 4"W x 5¾"L

Row 2:   **741.** Water Pitcher: Penguin, Multi-Color – 7¾"H

          742. Creamer: Platypus – 4"H

          743. Creamer: Pig, Gray – 4¼"H

          744. Creamer: Pig, Red – 4¼"H

          745. Milk Pitcher: Chamois, Stirrup – 5"H

Row 3:   **746.** Milk Pitcher: Monkey, Green – 4¾"H

          747. Creamer: Fox Head, Stirrup – 4 "H

          748. Cavalier Bust: 3¾"H

          749. Creamer: Kangaroo – 4¾"H

          750. Creamer: Ibex, Stirrup – 4"H

          751. Hat Pin Holder: Penguin – 5"H

Row 4:   **752.** Celery: Nautilus Shell, White Satin with Multi-Color on Nautilus, – 12"L

PAGE 77

Row 1:   **753.** Humidor with Lid: Art Nouveau Lady, White Satin Finish – 7"H

754. Dresser Tray: Art Nouveau Lady, White Satin Finish – 10"L x 7"W

755. Vase: Art Nouveau Lady, White Satin Finish – 7½"H x 5¼"W

Row 2: **756.** Wall Vase: Art Nouveau Lady, White Satin Finish – 8¾"H

757. Creamer: Art Nouveau Lady, Multi-Color, Very Colorful – 4"H

758. Vase: Art Nouveau Lady, White Satin Finish, Small – 5¼"H

759. Candlestick, Tall: Art Nouveau Lady, White Satin Finish, Handled – 6¼"H

Row 3: **760.** Candy Dish: Art Nouveau Lady in Drape, White Satin Finish – 6½"W

761. Pin Tray: Art Nouveau Lady in Drape, White Satin Finish, – 4½"W

762. Candlestick Holder: Art Nouveau, Short, White Satin Finish – 3"H x 5½"W

Row 4: **763.** Water Pitcher: Art Nouveau Lady, White Satin Finish – 6½"H

764. Milk Pitcher: Art Nouveau Lady, White Satin Finish – 4¾"H

765. Creamer: Art Nouveau Lady, White Satin Finish – 4"H

766. Sugar (with Lid): Art Nouveau Lady, White Satin Finish – 3"H

Row 5: **767.** Bowl: Art Nouveau Lady, White Satin, Oval Shape – 4½"H x 8"W

768. Box with Lid: Art Nouveau Lady, White Satin Finish – 1½"H x 5"L

769. Hanging Match Holder: Art Nouveau Lady, White Satin Finish – 4¾"H x 4"W

770. Bowl: Art Nouveau Lady, White Satin Finish – 3¼"H x 6"W

PAGE 78

Row 1: **771.** Humidor with Lid: Elk, (Handles are Two Heads) – 5½"H

772. Beer Mug (or Stein): Elk – 6"H

773. Water Pitcher: Elk – 7"H

774. Milk Pitcher: Elk – 5¼"H

775. Creamer: Elk – 4½"H

776. Candlestick Holders: Elk (Matching Pair) – 8"H

Row 2: **777.** Ink Well (with Lid): Elk – 6¼"L x 2⅞"H x 4½"W

778. Salt Shaker: Elk – 3"H

779. Candlestick Holder: Elk - Short Size – 7¼"L x 2½"H x 4⅜"W

780. Planter: Elk (Two Heads) – 9½"L x 6½"W

781. Ashtray: Elk – 6¼"L x 4½"W

782. Syrup (with Lid): Elk – 4½"H

783. Hanging Match Holder: Elk – 5"L

Row 3: **784.** Shaving Mug: Elk – 3½"L

785. Sugar with Lid: Elk (Handles are Two Heads), Short Size – 3"H

786. Pin Cushion: Elk – 3½"H

787. Sugar with Lid: Elk (Handles are Two Heads), Tall Size – 3¼"H

788. Toothpick Holder: Elk – 3"H

789. Cup (Stirrup): Elk – 4"H

790. Creamer (Stirrup): Elk – 4½"H

791. Milk Pitcher (Stirrup): Elk – 5½"H

Row 4: **792.** Match Holder: Elk – 4"H

793. Demi-Cup: Elk – 1¾"H, Saucer – 4"D

794. Celery: Elk, (Handles are Two Heads) – 12"L x 5"W

795. Relish: Elk – 9½"L x 4"W

796. Match Holder: Elk – 4"H

797. Toddy Cups: Elk – 2"H

PAGE 79

Row 1: 798. Creamer: Red Parrot Handle, White Pitcher – 5"H
799. Milk Pitcher: Green Parrot Handle, Ecru Pitcher – 6¾"H
800. Milk Pitcher: White Parrot Handle, Red Pitcher – 6¾"H
801. Milk Pitcher: Red Parrot Handle, Ecru Pitcher – 6¾H"
802. Water Pitcher: Red Parrot Handle, White Pitcher – 7¾"H

Row 2: 803. Humidor with Lid: Arab, Gray Turban – 4½"H
804. Shoe: Man's Brown High-Top, (Lace-up) – 3½"H
805. Shoe: Man's Tan Oxford – 5"L
806. Shoe: Man's Two-Tone Oxford (Right Foot) – 5"L
807. Shoe: Man's Two-Tone Oxford (Left Foot) – 5"L
808. Shoe: Man's Tan Oxford, (Toe Turned Up) – 5"L
809. Shoe: Man's Tan Oxford, Laces – 5"L
810. Shoe: Man's Tan and Brown High Lace – 2¾"H
811. Shoe: Man's Black High Lace (Back Tab) – 3¾"H
812. Humidor with Lid: Arab, White Turban – 4½"H

Row 3: 813. Milk Pitcher: White Cat Handle on Green Pitcher – 5"H
814. Creamer: Gray Brown Cat Handle on Blue Pitcher – 3¾"H
815. Creamer: Black Cat Handle on Ecru Pitcher – 4"H
816. Creamer: Monk – 4¼"H
817. Creamer: Man of the Mountain (Inscribed) – 3½"H

Row 4: 818. Creamer: Girl with Basket (Peach Dress) – 4"H
819. Shoe: Lady's Tan High-Top Lace (Original Laces) – 4"H
820. Shoe: Lady's Black High Lace – 3¾"H
821. Creamer: Milkmaid (Red Dress) – 4¾"H
822. High Top Shoe: Ladies' Two-Tone 3½"H
823. High Top Shoe: Ladies, Black – 3¾"H
824. Creamer: Girl with Pitcher (Blue Dress) – 4"H

PAGE 80

Row 1: 825. Water Pitcher: Clown, Red – 6½"H
826. Milk Pitcher: Clown, Red – 4½"H
827. Creamer: Clown, Red – 3¾"H
828. Mug: Clown, Red – 4½"H
829. Humidor with Lid: Lady Clown, Red, Small Size – 5"H x 4¾"W
830. Candlestick Holder: Clown, Red, Tall Size with Match Holder – 6¾"H
831. Humidor with Lid: Clown, Red, Large Size – 8"H

Row 2: 832. Candlestick: Clown, Red, Short Size – 6½"L x 3½"W
833. Powder Jar with Lid: Clown, Red – 4¼"H
834. Pipe rest: Clown, Red – 5¼"L x 2¾"H
835. Match Holder: Clown, Red – 3"H
836. Match Holder with Striker: Clown, Red – 4¼"L x 2½"H
837. Toothpick Holder: Clown, Red – 3"H
838. Salt Shaker: Clown, Red – 3¾"H
839. Ashtray: Clown, Red – 4½"L x 1¾"H
840. Hanging Match Holder: Clown, Red – 5"L

Row 3: 841. Candy Dish: Clown, Green – 7"L x 6¼"W
842. Ashtray: Clown, Green – 4½"L x 1¾"H

843. Pipe Rest: Clown, Yellow – 5¼"L x 2¾"W
844. Creamer: Clown, Yellow – 3¾"H
845. Milk Pitcher: Clown, Yellow – 4½"H
846. Water Pitcher: Clown, Yellow – 6½"H
Row 4: **847.** Match Holder: Clown, Black and Red – 3"H
848. Ashtray: Clown, White Satin Finish – 4½"L x 3½"W x 1¾"H
849. Creamer: Clown, Red – 3½"H

PAGE 81
Row 1: **850.** Water Pitcher: Bellringer – 7½"H
851. Humidor with Lid: Coachman – 7"H
852. Milk Pitcher: Coachman – 4¾"H
853. Creamer: Coachman – 4¼"H
854. Water Pitcher: Coachman – 7"H
855. Water Pitcher: Lamplighter – 7¾"H
Row 2: **856.** Milk Pitcher: Bellringer – 5"H
857. Creamer: Bellringer – 4½"H
858. Toothpick Holder: Bellringer – 3½"H
859. Toothpick Holder: Lamplighter – 3½"H
860. Creamer: Lamplighter – 4¾"H
861. Milk Pitcher: Lamplighter – 5¾"H
Row 3: **862.** Humidor with Lid: Lamplighter, Brown – 7¼"H
863. Toothpick Holder: Coachman – 3½"H
864. Salt and Pepper Shakers: Coachman – 2½"H
865. Toothpick Holder: Lamplighter – 3½"H
866. Ashtray: Chimpanzee – 5¼"L
867. Creamer: Chimpanzee – 4"H
868. Humidor with Lid: Chimpanzee – 5¾"H

PAGE 82
Row 1: **869.** Humidor with Lid: Devil and Cards – 7¼"H
870. Dresser Tray: Devil and Cards – 9¾"L x 7"W
871. Water Pitcher: Devil and Cards – 7¼"H
Row 2: **872.** Creamer: Devil and Cards – 3¾"H
873. Milk Pitcher: Devil and Cards – 5"H
874. Creamer: Devil and Cards – 3¾"H
875. Creamer: Devil and Cards, One Card – 3¾"H
Row 3: **876.** Hanging Wall Match Holder: Devil and Cards – 5"L x 4"W
877. Wall Match Holder: Devil and Cards, Full Body – 5¾"L x 4"W
878. Ashtray: Devil and Cards – 5"L x 4"W
Row 4: **879.** Card Box with Lid: Devil and Cards – 3½"L
880. Card Tray: Devil and Cards – 3¾"L x 3¾"W

PAGE 83
Row 1: **881.** Creamer: Red Devil – 3½"H
882. Mug: Devil and Cards (New Repro only made a few years in the 1940's. There is no blue rim around the top of the mug and the chin of the Devil is separated from the Mug) – 5"H

883. Candy Dish: Devil and Cards – 6½"D

884. Mug: Devil and Cards, (Old, has blue rim around the top and the Devil's chin is connected to the mug) – 5"H

885. Milk Pitcher: Red Devil – 4¼"H

Row 2: **886.** Sugar with Lid: Devil and Cards – 4"H

887. Sugar with Lid: Devil and Cards, Different Cards – 4"H

888. Ashtray: Devil and Cards (or Saucer for Demi-Cup) – 4"H

889. Salt and Pepper Shakers: Devil and Cards – 3"H

890. Open Sugar: Devil and Cards, Tall Size (Devil for Handles) – 3¾"H

Row 3: **891.** Ashtray: Red Devil – 2½"H x 4¾"L

892. Candlestick Holder: Devil and Cards – 3½"H x 6"L

893. Candlestick Holder: Devil and Cards – 2¼"H x 5"L

894. Candlestick Holder: Devil and Cards – 2¼"H x 5"L

895. Ashtray: Red Devil Head – 2½"H x 5½"L

Row 4: **896.** Devil and Dice Demi-Cup – 2¼"H

897. Demi-Cup: Devil and Dice, (Numbers Vary on Dice) – 2¼"H

898. Open Sugar: Devil and Cards – 2¾"H x 4"L

899. Toothpick Holder: Devil and Cards – 2½"H

PAGE 84

Row 1: **900.** Humidor: Santa Claus, Red, Small Size – 4¼"H

Row 2: **901.** Match Holder: Santa Claus, Strider on Pack, Red – 4¼"H

902. Creamer: Santa Claus, Green, Pack as Handle – 4"H

903. Candlestick Holder: Santa Claus, Red, Low Size – 4"W x 3"H

904. Lemonade Pitcher: Santa Claus, Pack as Handle, Red – 7¼"H

Row 3: **905.** Milk Pitcher: Santa Claus, Attached Handle, Brown – 5¼"H

906. Milk Pitcher: Santa Claus, Attached Handle, Red – 5¼"H

907. Milk Pitcher: Santa Claus, Attached Handle, Green – 5¼"H

908. Match Holder: Santa Claus, Striker on Pack, Red – 4¼"H

PAGE 85

Row 1: **909.** Candlestick: Santa Claus, Attached Handle, Red, Also Seen in Brown – 7½"H

910. Water Pitcher: Santa Claus, Pack as Handle, Red – 6⅛"H – (also in Brown)

911. Lemonade Pitcher: Santa Claus, Pack as Handle, Red – 7¼"H

912. Hanging Wall Vase or Pocket: Santa Claus, Full Figure, Red – 9"L

Row 2: **913.** Creamer: Santa Claus; Attached Handle, Brown – 4¼"H

914. Creamer: Santa Claus, Attached Handle, Red – 4¼"H

915. Milk Pitcher: Santa Claus, Attached Handle, Red – 5¼"H

916. Milk Pitcher: Santa Claus, Attached Handle, Green – 5¼"H

Row 3: **917.** Candy Dish: Santa Claus (Feet Base), Red (Also Seen In Brown) – 3¼"H x 4¾"W

918. Hanging Match Holder: Santa Claus, Green – 5¼"L

919. Ashtray: Santa Claus, Red – 1¾"H x 4¾"W

PAGE 86

Row 1: **920.** Hair Receiver (with Lid): Tapestry, Pink American Beauty Rose – 2¾"H x 4"W

921. Creamer: Tapestry, Pink American Beauty Rose, Pinched Spout – 3¼"H

922. Flower Pot or Planter (liner): Tapestry, Pink American Beauty Rose – 2¾"H

923. Tumbler: Tapestry, Pink American Beauty Rose – 3¾"H

Row 2: 924. Chocolate Set: Tapestry, Soft Yellow, White and Pink Roses Pot: – 8¾"H Cup: 3"H
Saucer: 4½"D

Row 3: 925. Miniature Ewer: Tapestry, Pink American Beauty Rose, Bulbous – 2½"H

926. Miniature Coal Scuttle: Tapestry, Pink American Beauty Rose – 3"H

927. Creamer: Tapestry, Pink American Beauty Rose, Corset Shape – 3½"H

928. Shoe (Low Cut): Tapestry, Pink American Beauty Rose – 2½"H

Row 4: 929. Bell: Tapestry, Pink American Beauty Rose, (Lime Green Background) – 3"H

930. Vase: Tapestry, Sterling Silver Roses (Rare Color) – 3¾"H

931. Milk Pitcher: Tapestry, Sterling Silver Roses (Rare Color), Pinched Spout – 5"H

932. Basket: Tapestry, Sterling Silver Roses (Rare Color), Pinched Spout – 3¼"H x 4¼"L

PAGE 87

Row 1: 933. Plate: Tapestry, Dark Orange-Gold and Pink Roses, Scroll Rim – 9½"D

934. Plate: Tapestry, Dark Orange-Gold and Pink Roses, Gold Scroll Rim – 9½"D

935. Vase: Tapestry, Dark Orange-Gold and Pink Roses – 5¼"H

936. Vase: Tapestry, Dark Orange-Gold and Pink Roses, Gold Handles – 5¾"H

937. Water Pitcher: Tapestry, Dark Orange-Gold and Pink Roses, Pinched Spout, 6"H

Row 2: 938. Dresser Tray: Tapestry, Rose and Daisy (Very Busy), – 11"L x 8"W

939. Water Pitcher: Tapestry, Rose and Daisy (Very Busy), Pinched Spout – 6"H

940. Bowl: Tapestry, Rose and Daisy (Very Busy), Shell and Leaf Mold – 10½"D

Row 3: 941. Hair Receiver: Tapestry, Napoleonic Couple (Lady Seated) and Roses, Footed – 2½"H

942. Shoe: Tapestry, Napoleonic Couple (Hand in Tunic) and Roses – 2½"H

943. Powder Jar (Lid): Tapestry, Napoleonic Couple (Lady Seated) and Roses, Footed – 2½"H

944. Vase: Tapestry, Rose and Daisy (Very Busy) – 4½"H

945. Flower Pot or Planter (liner): Tapestry, Rose and Daisy (Very Busy) Gold Handles – 2¾"H

Row 4: 946. Hatpin Holder: Tapestry, Pink Border Roses with White and Cream Center Roses,
Reticulated Base – 4½"H

947. Creamer: Tapestry, Rose and Daisy (Very Busy), Pinched Spout – 3¼"H

948. Milk Pitcher: Tapestry, Rose and Daisy (Very Busy), Pinched Spout, – 5"H

949. Basket: Tapestry, Napoleonic Couple and Roses, Ruffled, with Ornate Handle – 5"H

950. Wall Vase: Tapestry, Napoleonic Couple (Hand in Tunic) and Roses – 9"L

PAGE 88

Row 1: 951. Vase: Tapestry, Japanese Chrysanthemum (Rare Flower), Reverse Cone Shape – 6¾"H

952. Plate: Tapestry, Japanese Chrysanthemum, Open Handled – 10½"D

953. Basket: Tapestry, Japanese Chrysanthemum, Gold Handle – 7"H

954. Plate: Tapestry, Japanese Chrysanthemum, Shell and Leaf Mold – 7½"D

Row 2: 955. Dresser Tray: Tapestry, Japanese Chrysanthemum – 9¾"L x 7"W

956. Teapot: Tapestry, Japanese Chrysanthemum, Gold, Square Handle – 4¾"H

957. Dish: Tapestry, Japanese Chrysanthemum, Leaf Shape – 5"W

958. Dish: Tapestry, Mums, Leaf Shape – 7"H x 6½"W

Row 3: 959. Dish (or Shallow Basket): Tapestry, Japanese Chrysanthemum, Handled – 8"L x 4"W
x 4"H

960. Ashtray: Tapestry, Japanese Chrysanthemum, Square Shape – 4"L x 4"W

961. Dish (or Shallow Basket): Tapestry, Mums, Handled – 8¼"L x 4"W x 4"H

Row 4: 962. Mug: Tapestry, Japanese Chrysanthemum – 3¼"H

963. Creamer: Tapestry, Japanese Chrysanthemum, Gold, Square Handle – 4"H

964. Powder Jar (with Lid): Tapestry, Mums, Footed – 2¼"H x 4"W

965. Powder Jar (with Lid): Tapestry, Mums, Very Rare – 3¼"H x 6"W

PAGE 89

Row 1: **966.** Plate: Tapestry, Lady with Horse (Leaning on Left Arm) – 9½"D

967. Vase: Tapestry, Lady with Horse (Leaning on Left Arm) – 9"H

968. Vase: Tapestry, Lady with Horse (Leaning on Right Arm), Ornate Handle – 9"H

969. Plate: Tapestry, Lady with Horse (Leaning on Right Arm), Scroll Rim – 9½"D (These pieces may be signed by German Artist, "Wagner")

Row 2: **970.** Humidor (with Lid): Tapestry, Lady with Horse (Leaning on Right Arm) – 6½"H

971. Milk Pitcher: Tapestry, Lady with Horse (Leaning on Left Arm), Pinched Spout – 5"H

972. Charger Plate: Tapestry, Stag in Stream and Gazebo, Scroll Rim – 11½"D

973. Vase: Tapestry, Stag in Stream and Gazebo – 9"H

Row 3: **974.** Vase: Tapestry, Lady with Horse (Leaning on Right Arm), Very Rare – 7"H

975. Miniature Ewer: Tapestry, Lady with Horse (Leaning on Left Arm) – 2½"H

976. Vase: Tapestry, Lady with Horse (Leaning on Right Arm), Ruffled Top, Footed, Handles – 4½"H

977. Toothpick Holder: Tapestry, Lady with Horse (Leaning on Left Arm), Bucket Shape with Handle – 3"H

978. Creamer: Tapestry, Lady with Horse (Leaning on Right Arm), Corset Shape, Pinched Spout – 3½"H

979. Bell: Tapestry, Lady with Horse (Leaning on Right Arm) – 3"H

980. Vase: Tapestry, Stag in Stream and Gazebo, Ornate Handled – 5¾"H

981. Vase: Tapestry, Stag in Stream and Gazebo, Handles – 5¾"H

982. Creamer: Tapestry, Stag in Stream and Gazebo, Pinched Spout – 4"H

Row 4: **983.** Hanging Match Holder: Tapestry, Lady with Horse (Leaning on Left Arm) – 4½"H

984. Toothpick Holder: Tapestry, Lady with Horse (Leaning on Right Arm), Footed, Handled – 2¾"H

985. Miniature Coal Scuttle: Tapestry, Lady with Horse (Leaning on Left Arm) – 3"H

986. Vase: Tapestry, Stag in Stream and Gazebo, Footed, Handled and Ruffled – 4¼"H

987. Toothpick Holder: Tapestry, Stag in Stream and Gazebo, Footed, with Handle (Ad Piece, Gettysburg 1863) – 2¾"H

988. Vase: Tapestry, Stag in Stream and Gazebo, Handles – 4¼"H

989. Vase: Tapestry, Stag in Stream and Gazebo, Bulbous, Stick Spout – 4"H

PAGE 90

Row 1: **990.** Vase: Tapestry, Light Yellow Rose, Reverse Cone Shape – 4¼"H

991. Powder Jar (with Lid): Tapestry, Light Yellow Rose, Large Size – 4"H x 6½"W

992. Hair Receiver (with Lid): Tapestry, Light Yellow Rose, Footed – 2½"H x 4"W

993. Box (with Lid): Tapestry, Light Yellow Rose, Triangle Shape, – 1¾"H x 2¼"W

994. Ash Tray: Tapestry, Light Yellow Rose, Triangle Shape – 5" x 5"

995. Basket: Tapestry, Light Yellow Rose, Gold Handle – 6¾"H x 3½"W x 7¼"L

Row 2: **996.** Basket: Tapestry, Violets, Gold Handle – 4"H x 4½"L x 2½"W

997. Shoe: Tapestry (Low Cut); Violets – 2½"H

998. Hatpin Holder: Tapestry, Violets, Reticulated Base – 4¾"H

999. Vase (or Toothbrush Holder): Tapestry, Violets – 4¼"H

1000. Dresser Tray: Tapestry, Violets – 10"L x 7¼"W

1001. Pin Box (with Lid): Tapestry, Violets – 2"H x 3½"L x 2¼"W

1002. Pin Box (With Lid): Tapestry, Violets – 1¾"H x 4½"L x 2½"W

1003. Powder Jar (with Lid): Tapestry, Violets – 2¼"H x 3½"W

1004. Dish (with Lid): Tapestry, Violets, Three Feet, 2½"H x 4¼"W

Row 3: **1005.** Milk Pitcher: Tapestry, Pink Rose with Green Background, Pinched Spout – 5"H

1006. Shoe Pin Cushion: Tapestry, Pink Rose with Green Background (Original) – 2½"

1007. Basket: Tapestry, Pink Rose with Green Background, Gold Handle – 6½"H x 7"L

1008. Pin Box (with Lid): Tapestry, Pink Rose with Green Background – 2"H x 4"L x 2"W

1009. Basket: Tapestry, Pink Rose with Green Background, Gold Handle – 4"H x 4"L

Row 4: **1010.** Vase: Tapestry, Pink Rose with Green Background, Bulbous, Stick Spout – 4"H

1011. Basket: Tapestry, Pink Rose with Green Background, Gold Handle – 4½"H

1012. Planter or Flower Pot with Insert: Tapestry, Pink Rose with Green Background, Handled – 2¾"H

1013. Creamer: Tapestry, Pink Rose with Green Background, Corset Shape with Pinched Spout – 3¾"H

PAGE 91

Row 1: **1014.** Water Pitcher: Tapestry, Castle by the Lake, Pinched Spout, Rare – 6½"H

1015. Vase: Tapestry, Castle by the Lake, Bulbous, Stick Spout – 5"H

1016. Toothpick Holder: Tapestry, Castle by the Lake, Knob Handles – 2¾"H

1017. Tumbler: Tapestry, Castle by the Lake – 3¾"H

1018. Hanging Match Holder: Tapestry, Cottage by the Water Fall – 4½"H

1019. Miniature Creamer: Tapestry, Cottage by the Water Fall – 2¾"H

1020. Pin Box (with Lid): Tapestry, Cottage by the Water Fall – 1¾"H x 4¼"L

1021. Milk Pitcher: Tapestry, Cottage by the Water Fall, Pinched Spout – 4¾"H

1022. Nappy: Tapestry, Cottage by the Water Fall, Clover Shape – 4¼"L

1023. Charger Plate: Tapestry, Cottage by the Water Fall, Gold Scroll Rim, Very Rare – 11½"D

Row 2: **1024.** Dresser Tray: Tapestry, Castle by the Lake – 11½"L x 8"W

1025. Vase: Tapestry, The Bathers (Castle in Background), Stick Spout, Rare – 8¼"H

1026. Water Pitcher: Tapestry, The Bathers (Castle in Background), Pinched Spout – 6½"H

1027. Vase: Tapestry, The Bathers (Castle in Background), Bulbous, Stick Spout – 7½"H

Row 3: **1028.** Vase: Tapestry, Castle by the Lake, Bulbous, Stick Spout – 5"H

1029. Bell: Tapestry, Castle by the Lake – 3¼"H

1030. Stamp Box (with Lid): Tapestry, Castle by the Lake, Dividers in Base – 3½"L x 1¾"W

1031. Miniature Watering Can: Tapestry, The Bathers (Castle in the Background) Rare – 2¾"H

1032. Tumbler: Tapestry, The Bathers (Castle in the Background) – 4"H

1033. Milk Pitcher: Tapestry, The Bathers (Castle in the Background), Pinched Spout – 4¾"H

Row 4: **1034.** Miniature Ewer: Tapestry, The Bathers (Castle in the Background) – 3"H

1035. Vase: Tapestry, The Bathers (Castle in the Background), Footed with Handles and Ruffled Top – 4¼"H

1036. Vase: Tapestry, The Bathers (Castle in the Background), Stick Spout – 4½"H

1037. Creamer: Tapestry, The Bathers (Castle in the Background), Pinched Spout – 4"H

1038. Creamer: Tapestry, The Bathers (Castle in the Background), Pinched Spout – 3½"H

PAGE 92

1039. Vase (or Toothbrush Holder): Tapestry, Christmas Cactus – 4½"H

1040. Powder Jar (with Lid): Tapestry, Christmas Cactus – 2½"H x 3½"W

1041. Clock: Tapestry, Christmas Cactus, Very Rare – 4½"H

1042. Dresser Tray: Tapestry, Christmas Cactus – 11"L x 8"W

Row 2: **1043.** Basket: Tapestry, Orange-Gold Rose, Gold Handle, Rare – 5 "H x 6½"L x 4"W

1044. Toothpick Holder: Tapestry, Orange-Gold, Rose, Bucket Shape, Handle – 3"H

1045. Ring Holder (Ring-Tree): Tapestry, Christmas Cactus – 3½"W

1046. Vase (Matching Pair): Tapestry, Christmas Cactus – 5"H

1047. Hair Receiver with Lid: Tapestry, Christmas Cactus, Footed – 2½"H x 4½"W

1048. Hatpin Holder: Tapestry, Christmas Cactus, Reticulated Base – 4¾"H

Row 3 **1049.** Basket: Tapestry, Orange-Gold Rose, Handle – 4½"H x 3½"L

1050. Basket: Tapestry, Orange-GoldRose, Handle – 4½"H

1051. Flower Pot or Planter (Liner): Tapestry, Orange-Gold Rose, Handle – 2¾"H x 3"W

1052. Sugar Shaker (Cork Bottom): Tapestry, Orange-Gold Rose, Reticulated Base – 4½"H

1053. Basket: Tapestry, Orange-Gold Rose, Handle – 5½"H x 4¼"L x 3"W

Row 4: **1054.** Toothpick Holder: Tapestry, Rose with Ivy Border, Three-Hole (Rare) – 3"H

1055. Pin Box (with Lid): Tapestry, Rose with Ivy Border – 1¾"H x 4½"L x 2½"W

1056. Creamer: Tapestry, Rose with Ivy Border, (Corset Shape) – 3¾"H

1057. Vase: Tapestry, Rose with Ivy Border – 4"H

PAGE 93

Row 1: **1058.** Dresser Tray: Tapestry, Highland Sheep – 11"L x 8"W

1059. Hanging Match Holder: Tapestry, Highland Sheep – 4½"L

1060. Creamer: Tapestry, Highland Sheep, Corset Shape and Pinched Spout – 3¾"H

1061. Powder Jar (with Lid): Tapestry, Brown and White Cows (Facing East), Footed – 2½"H x 4"W

1062. Planter or Flower Pot (Liner Not Shown): Tapestry, Brown and White Cows (Facing West) – 3"H

1063. Relish: Tapestry, Arab on Brown Horse – 7½"L x 4¾"W

1064. Nappy: Tapestry, Arab on White Horse, Leaf Shape – 4½"W

Row 2: **1065.** Humidor (with Lid): Tapestry, Cow (Black), Rare – 6½"H

1066. Miniature Ewer: Tapestry, Cow (Black) – 2¾"H

1067. Bell: Tapestry, Cow (Black) – 3¼"H

1068. Vase: Tapestry, Cow (Black), Bulbous, Stick Spout – 4"H

1069. Vase: Tapestry, Cow (Black), Footed, Handled, Ruffled Top – 4¼"H

1070. Miniature Pitcher: Tapestry, Cow (Black) – 2¾"H

1071. Hatpin Holder: Tapestry, Cow (Black), Reticulated Base – 4½"H

Row 3: **1072.** Creamer: Tapestry, Highland Goats, Corset Shape, Pinched Spout – 3¾"H

1073. Miniature Pitcher: Tapestry, Highland Goats – 3½"H

1074. Creamer: Tapestry, Highland Goats, Pinched Spout – 4"H

1075. Miniature Sofa (Very Rare): Tapestry, Highland Goats, Footed, Gold Scroll Border – 3¼"H x 4½"L

1076. Ashtray: Tapestry, Highland Goats, Triangle Shape – 5" x 5"

Row 4: **1077.** Salt and Pepper Shakers: Tapestry, Highland Goats – 2¾"H

1078. Pin Box (with Lid): Tapestry, Highland Goats – 1½"H x 2½"L

1079. Hair Receiver: Tapestry, Highland Goats, Footed – 2½"H x 4"W

PAGE 94

1080. Picture Frame: Tapestry, Double Pink Rose, Very Rare – 8¼"L x 6"W

1081. Picture Frame: Tapestry, Double Pink Rose, Rare – 5½"L x 4¼"W

1082. Plate: Tapestry, Double Pink Rose, Shell and Leaf Mold – 7½"D
1083. Water Pitcher: Tapestry, Double Pink Rose, Square Handle, Alligator Mouth, Rare – 5¾"H

Row 2: 1084. Milk Pitcher: Tapestry, Double Pink Rose, Square Handle, Alligator Mouth, Rare – 4½"H
1085. Vase: Tapestry, Double Pink Rose, Handle and Ruffled Top – 4"H
1086. Pin Box (with Lid): Tapestry, Double Pink Rose – 1¾"H x 4"L
1087. Basket: Tapestry, Double Pink Rose, Reticulated Base with Handle – 5"H x 5"L x 3¾"W
1088. Hair Receiver (with Lid): Tapestry, Double Pink Rose, Footed – 2¾"H x 4"W
1089. Vase: Tapestry, Double Pink Rose, Ornate Handles – 5¾"H
1090. Shoe (Low-Cut): Tapestry, Double Pink Rose – 2½"H
1091. Basket: Tapestry, Double Pink Rose, Handle and Ruffled Top – 5"H x 5"W

Row 3: 1092. Candy Dish: Tapestry, Double Pink Rose, Leaf Shape – 5"L
1093. Planter or Flower Pot: Tapestry, Double Pink Rose (Liner Not Shown) – 2½"H
1094. Basket: Tapestry, Double Pink Rose, Handle, (Roses Inside Basket) – 4"H x 4½"L x 2½"W
1095. Creamer: Tapestry, Double Pink Rose, Square Handle, Alligator Mouth, Rare – 3"H
1096. Ashtray: Tapestry, Double Pink Rose, Square Shape – 5¾" x 5¾"

Row 4: 1097. Hatpin Holder: Tapestry, Rose and Daisy, Reticulated Base – 4½"H
1098. Creamer: Tapestry, Double Pink Rose, Pinched Spout – 3½"H
1099. Toothpick Holder: Tapestry, Double Pink Rose, Handles, Footed – 2¾"H
1100. Salt and Pepper Shakers: Tapestry, Double Pink Rose – 3¼"H
1101. Wall Match Holder: Tapestry, Double Pink Rose – 4½"L

PAGE 95

Row 1: 1102. Plate: Tapestry, Toaster Cavalier (Stein Extended), Gold Scrolling – 9½"D
1103. Basket: Tapestry, Toaster Cavalier (Stein Extended), Gold Handle – 5½"H x 6½"W
1104. Vase: Tapestry, Toaster Cavalier (Stein Extended), Bulbous, Stick Spout – 6"H
1105. Humidor (with Lid): Tapestry, Toaster Cavalier (Stein Extended), Rare – 6½"H
1106. Hanging Match Holder: Tapestry, Toaster Cavalier (Stein Extended) – 4½"L
1107. Miniature Ewer: Tapestry, Toaster Cavalier (Stein Extended) – 2½"H
1108. Vase: Tapestry, Toaster Cavalier (Stein Extended) – 4"H

Row 2: 1109. Dresser Tray: Tapestry, Cavalier Musicians (Mandolin) Some are artist signed "Dixon" – 11"L x 7¾"W
1110. Vase: Tapestry, Cavalier Musician, (Mandolin) Handled, Rare– 8"H
1111. Dresser Tray: Tapestry, Toaster Cavalier (Stein Extended) – 11"L x 7¾"H

Row 3: 1112. Creamer: Tapestry, Cavalier Musicians, (Mandolin), Pinched Spout – 4"H
1113. Vase: Tapestry, Cavalier Musicians(Mandolin), Handled – 4½"H
1114. Miniature Coal Scuttle: Tapestry, Cavalier Musicians (Mandolin) – 3"H
1115. Creamer: Tapestry, Cavalier Musicians, (Mandolin), Corset Shape – 3½"H
1116. Vase: Tapestry, Cavalier Musicians (Mandolin) – 3¾"H
1117. Powder Jar (with Lid): Tapestry, Cavalier Musicians (Mandolin), Footed – 2¼"H x 4"W

Row 4: 1118. Creamer: Tapestry, Pheasant, Pinched Spout – 4"H
1119. Nappy: Tapestry, Pheasant, Leaf Shape – 4½"L
1120. Vase: Tapestry, Pheasant, Ornate Handle – 5½"H
1121. Pin Box (with Lid): Tapestry, Pheasant – 1¾"H x 4½"L

1122. Vase: Tapestry, Pheasant, Bulbous, Stick Spout – 4"H

PAGE 96
Row 1: **1123.** Plate: Tapestry, Double White Rose with Pink Roses, Gold Scroll Rim – 9"D
1124. Chocolate Pot (with Lid): Tapestry, Double White Rose with Pink Roses, Footed – 9"H
1125. Creamer: Tapestry, Double White Rose with Pink Roses, Pinched Spout – 4"H
1126. Hanging Match Holder: Tapestry, Double White Rose with Pink Roses – 4½"L
1127. Hanging Match Holder: Tapestry, Pink and Yellow Rose – 4½"L
1128. Nappy: Tapestry, Double White Rose with Pink Roses, Leaf Shape – 4½"L
1129. Powder Jar (with Lid): Tapestry, Double White Rose with Pink Roses, Footed – 2½"H

Row 2: **1130.** Vase: Tapestry, Pink Border Roses with White and Cream Center Rose, Bulbous – 3½"H
1131. Creamer: Tapestry, Pink Border Roses with White and Cream Center Rose, Corset Shape – 4"
1132. Pin Box (with Lid): Tapestry, Pink Border Roses with White and Cream Center Rose – 1¾"H x 4¾"L
1133. Clock: Tapestry, Pink Border Roses with White and Cream Center Rose – 4½"H
1134. Vases: (Matching Pair): Tapestry, Pink Border Roses with White and Cream Center Rose – 4½"H
1135. Vases (Matching Pair): Tapestry, Vertical Pink Rose Column (One has Smaller Base) – 4"H
1136. Vases (Matching Pair): Tapestry, Vertical Pink Rose Column – 6½"H

Row 3: **1137.** Nappy: Tapestry, Pink Border Roses with White and Cream Center Roses, Leaf Shape – 4½"L
1138. Basket: Tapestry, Pink Border Roses with White and Cream Center Roses – 4"H
1139. Ring Tree: Tapestry, Pink Border Roses with White and Cream Center Roses – 3½"D
1140. Ring Tree: Tapestry, Pink Border Roses with White and Cream Center Roses (One Single Twisted Center Prong) – 3½"D
1141. Candy Dish: Tapestry, Pink Border Roses with White and Cream Center Roses, Leaf Shape – 5"L
1142. Vase: Tapestry, Pink Border Roses with White and Cream Center Roses – 4¾"H

Row 4: **1143.** Box (with Lid): Tapestry, Pink Border Roses with White and Cream Center Roses, Shell Shape – 2"H x 5¼"W
1144. Box (with Lid): Tapestry, Pink Border Roses with White and Cream Center Roses – 1¾"H x 3½"W
1145. Box (with Lid): Tapestry, Pink Border Roses with White and Cream Center Roses, Very Rare – 2"H x 5"W
1146. Shoes: Tapestry, Pink Border Roses with White and Cream Center Roses, Matching Left and Right, Low Cut – 2¾"H
1147. Vase: Tapestry, Pink Border Roses with White and Cream Center Roses – 4"H

PAGE 97
Row 1: **1148.** Plate: Tapestry, Shawl Lady, Gold Scroll Rim, Very Rare – 9½"D
1149. Vase: Tapestry, Shawl Lady, Gold Handles – 5½"H
1150. Dessert Dish: Tapestry, Shawl Lady, Shell and Leaf Mold – 5¾"D

1151. Creamer: Tapestry, Shawl Lady, Corset Shape – 3½"H

1152. Miniature Coal Scuttle: Tapestry, Shawl Lady – 3¼"H

1153. Creamer: Tapestry, Shawl Lady, Pinched Spout – 3½"H

Row 2: 1154. Milk Pitcher: Tapestry, Muff Lady, Pinched Spout – 4¼"H

1155. Vase: Tapestry, Muff Lady, Gold Handles, Very Rare – 9½"H

1156. Vase: Tapestry, Muff Lady – 6"H

1157. Vase: Tapestry, Muff Lady, Bulbous, Stick Spout – 5"H

1158. Vase: Tapestry, Muff Lady, Very Rare – 7"H

Row 3: 1159. Creamer: Tapestry, Muff Lady, Pinched Spout – 3½"H

1160. Toothpick Holder: Tapestry, Muff Lady, Footed, Knob Handles – 2¾"H

1161. Bell: Tapestry, Muff Lady – 3¼"H

1162. Powder Jar (with Lid): Tapestry, Muff Lady, Footed – 2½"H x 4"W

1163. Miniature Vase: Tapestry, Muff Lady, Gold Handles – 3"H

1164. Vase: Tapestry, Muff Lady, Footed, Ruffled Top with Gold Handles – 4½"H

Row 4: 1165. Creamer: Tapestry, The Peering Lady (Hand Shielding Eyes), Pinched Spout – 3½"H

1166. Hanging Match Holder: Tapestry, The Peering Lady (Hand Shielding Eyes) – 4½"L

1167. Toothpick Holder: Tapestry, The Peering Lady (Hand Shielding Eyes), Knob Handles – 2¾"H

1168. Cracker Jar (with Lid): Tapestry, The Peering Lady (Hand Shielding Eyes), Very Rare – 6"H

PAGE 98

Row 1: 1169. Dresser Tray: Tapestry, Pink Border Roses with White and Cream Center Roses – 11½"L x 8"W

1170. Lemonade Pitcher: Tapestry, Pink Border Roses with White and Cream Center Roses, Corset Shape, Very Rare – 8"H

1171. Bowl: Tapestry, Pink Border Rose with White and Cream Center Roses, (Master Size), Shell and Leaf Mold – 10½"D

Row 2: 1172. Creamer: Tapestry, Pink Border Roses with White and Cream Center Roses, Corset Shape – 3¾"H

1173. Sugar (with Lid): Tapestry, Pink Border Roses with White and Cream Center Roses, Square Handle – 3"H

1174. Toothpick Holder: Tapestry, Pink Border Roses with White and Cream Center Roses, Footed, with Gold Handle – 2¾"H

1175. Toothpick Holder: Tapestry, Pink Border Roses with White and Cream Center Roses, Gold Handle – 3¼"H

1176. Teapot (with Lid): Tapestry, Pink Border Roses with White and Cream Center Roses, Square Handle – 4½"H

1177. Powder Jar (with Lid): Tapestry, Pink Border Roses with White and Cream Center Roses – 2"H x 3"W

1178. Basket: Tapestry, Pink Border Roses with White and Cream Center Roses, Handle, Rare – 4"H x 4"W

1179. Pin Box (with Lid): Tapestry, Pink Border Roses with White and Cream Center Roses – 3½"H

1180. Vase: Tapestry, Pink Border Roses with White and Cream Center Roses – 5"H

Row 3: 1181. Creamer: Tapestry, Pink Border Roses with White and Cream Center Roses, Square Handle (Goes with Sugar and Teapot Above) – 3"H

1182. Vase: Tapestry, Pink Border Roses, with White and Cream Center Roses, Stick Spout – 4½"H

1183. Basket: Tapestry, Pink Border Roses with White and Cream Center Roses, Handle – 4½"H

1184. Mug: Tapestry, Pink Border Roses with White and Cream Center Roses, Square Gold Handle, Rare – 4½"H

1185. Vase (or Toothbrush Holder): Tapestry, Pink Border Roses with White and Cream Center Roses – 4¼"H

Row 4: **1186.** Box (with Lid): Tapestry, Pink Border Roses with White and Cream Roses – 4"H

1187. Powder Jar (with Lid): Tapestry, Pink Border Roses with White and Cream Roses, Rare – 2½"H x 3"W

1188. Dessert Size Dish (to Master Bowl Above): Tapestry, Pink Border Roses with White and Cream Roses, Shell and Leaf Mold – 6"D

1189. Planter or Flower Pot (Liner Not Shown): Tapestry, Pink Border Roses with White and Cream Roses – 3"H

PAGE 99

Row 1: **1190.** Vase: Tapestry, Swans on Lake, Ornate Handle, Rare – 8"H

1191. Wall Vase or Pocket: Tapestry, Lady Feeding Chickens – 8¾"H

1192. Vase: Tapestry, The Chase (Hounds and Stag in Stream), Miniature, Ornate Handle – 3"H

1193. Vase: Tapestry, The Chase (Hounds and Stag in Stream), Rare – 7¾"H

1194. Dresser Tray: Tapestry, Colonial Curtsy Scene – 11¾"L x 8¼"W

Row 2: **1195.** Dish: Tapestry, Colonial Curtsy Scene, Leaf Shape – 5"L

1196. Hair Receiver: Tapestry, Colonial Curtsy Scene, Footed – 2½"H x 4"W

1197. Powder Jar (with Lid): Tapestry, Colonial Curtsy Scene, Footed – 2"H x 4"W

1198. Sugar (with Lid): Tapestry, Colonial Curtsy Scene – 2¾"H

1199. Pin Tray: Tapestry, Colonial Curtsy Scene – 5"L x 3½"W

1200. Pin Box (with Lid): Tapestry, Colonial Curtsy Scene – 2"H x 3¼"L

1201. Vase: Tapestry, Colonial Curtsy Scene – 4"H

1202. Shoe: Tapestry, Colonial Curtsy Scene, Low Cut, Original Lace; Rare – 2¾"H

Row 3: **1203.** Vase: Tapestry, Peacock, Handled – 4½"H

1204. Vase: Tapestry, Peacock, Ornate Handles – 5¼"H

1205. Vase: Tapestry, Polar Bear, Bulbous Shape with Stick Spout, Very Rare – 3½"H

1206. Vase: Tapestry, Polar Bear, Handled, Very Rare – 4¼"H

1207. Vase: Tapestry, Swan, Ornate Handles – 5½"H

1208. Hair Receiver: Tapestry, Swan, Footed – 2½"H x 4"W

1209. Creamer: Tapestry, Swans, Pinched Spout – 4"H

Row 4: **1210.** Nappy: Tapestry, Swan, Leaf Shape – 4½"L

1211. Miniature Coal Scuttle: Tapestry, Swan – 3"H

1212. Miniature Ewer: Tapestry, Swan – 2¾"H

1213. Toothpick Holder: Tapestry, Swan, Footed, Knob Handled – 3"H

1214. Miniature Watering Can: Tapestry, Swan, (Right-Handed), Very Rare – 2¾"H

1215. Miniature Pitcher: Tapestry, Swan – 2¼"H

1216. Miniature Watering Can: Tapestry, Swan, (Left-Handed), Very Rare – 2¾"H

1217. Miniature Vase: Tapestry, Swan – 3¼"H

PAGE 100

Row 1: **1218.** Dish: Tapestry, White Rose, Leaf Shape – 5"L

1219. Vase: Tapestry, White Rose – 6½"H

1220. Hanging Wall Vase or Pocket: Tapestry, White Rose – 8¾"L

1221. Vase: Tapestry, White Rose – 6½"H

1222. Dish: Tapestry, White Rose, Leaf Shape – 5"W

Row 2: **1223.** Basket: Tapestry, White Rose, Handle – 5¾"H x 6¾"W

1224. Basket: Tapestry, White Rose, Handle – 4¾"H x 5¼"W

1225. Basket: Tapestry, White Rose, Handle – 3¾"H x 4¼"H

1226. Salt (Large Holes) and Pepper (Small Holes) Shakers: Tapestry, White Rose – 3¼"H

1227. Cracker Jar (with Lid): Tapestry, White Rose, Knob Handles – 5"H

1228. Sugar (with Lid): Tapestry, White Rose, Square Handle – 3¼"H

1229. Creamer: Tapestry, White Rose, Square Handle – 3"H

Row 3: **1230.** Hanging Match Holder: Tapestry, White Rose – 4½"L

1231. Nut Bowl Set: Tapestry, White Rose, Footed, Master – 3"H x 6"W; Small, Rare – 1½"H x 3"W

1232. Flower Pot or Planter (Liner Not Shown): Tapestry, White Rose – 2¾"H

Row 4: **1233.** Relish: Tapestry, White Rose, Gold Rim, Open Handle – 8"L x 4"W

1234. Powder Jar (with Lid): Tapestry, White Rose – 2"H x 3"W

1235. Plate: Tapestry, White Rose, Shell and Leaf Mold – 6"D

1236. Bell: Tapestry, White Rose, Rare – 3¼"H

1237. Relish: Tapestry, White Rose, Gold Scroll Rim – 8"L x 4¾"W

PAGE 101

Row 1: **1238.** Plate: Tapestry, White Rose, Dinner or Cake Size, Open Handle – 10½"D

1239. Plate: Tapestry, White Rose, Shell and Leaf Mold – 7½"D

1240. Vase: Tapestry, White Rose, Reverse Cone Shape – 4"H

1241. Vase: Tapestry, White Rose, Reverse Cone Shape – 5"H

1242. Humidor (with Lid): Tapestry, White Rose, Very Rare – 6¾"H x 4¼"W

Row 2: **1243.** Creamer: Tapestry, White Rose, Pinched Spout – 4½"H

1244. Creamer: Tapestry, White Rose, Pinched Spout – 3¼"H

1245. Flower Pot or Planter (Liner): Tapestry, White Rose – 3"H

1246. Hatpin Holder: Tapestry, White Rose, Reticulated Base – 4½"H

1247. Powder Jar (with Lid): Tapestry, White Rose, Footed – 2½"H x 4"W

1248. Dresser Tray: Tapestry, White Rose – 11"L x 8"W

1249. Hair Receiver (with Lid Not Shown): Tapestry, White Rose, Footed – 2½"H x 4"W

1250. Vase: Tapestry, White Rose – 4¾"H

Row 3: **1251.** Candlestick Holder: Tapestry, White Rose, Rare – 4¼"H

1252. Shoe: Tapestry, White Rose, High-Cut, Rare – 3½"H

1253. Shoe: Tapestry, White Rose, Low-Cut – 2½"H

1254. Creamer: Tapestry, White Rose, Corset Shape – 3¾"H

1255. Milk Pitcher: Tapestry, White Rose, Corset Shape – 4¾"H

Row 4: **1256.** Basket: Tapestry, White Rose, Footed, Reticulated Base and Handle – 5¾"H x 5"W

1257. Box with Lid: Tapestry, White Rose, Square Shape – 2½" x 2½"

1258. Pin Box (with Lid): Tapestry, White Rose, Oval Shape – 1¾"H x 4½"L

1259. Toothpick Holder: Tapestry, White Rose, Bucket Shape with Handle – 3"H

1260. Toothpick Holder: Tapestry, White Rose, Handles, Footed – 2½"H

PAGE 102

Row 1: **1261.** Dresser Tray: Tapestry, Triple Pink Roses (in Center) – 11"L x 8"W

1262. Plate: Tapestry, Triple Pink Roses, Shell and Leaf Mold – 6"D

1263. Plate: Tapestry, Triple Pink Roses, Shell and Leaf Mold – 7½"D

1264. Plate: Tapestry, Triple Pink Roses, Cake Size, Open Handle – 10½"D

Row 2: **1265.** Chocolate Pot (with Lid): Tapestry, Triple Pink Roses, Footed – 8½"H

1266. Bowl: Tapestry, Triple Pink Roses, Shell and Leaf Mold – 10½"D

1267. Creamer: Tapestry, Triple Pink Roses, Corset Shape – 4¾"H

1268. Milk Pitcher: Tapestry, Triple Pink Roses, Corset Shape – 5¾"H

Row 3: **1269.** Flower Pot or Planter: Tapestry, Triple Pink Roses, (Liner Not Shown) – 3"H x 4"D

1270. Basket: Tapestry, Triple Pink Roses – 3¾"H x 4¼"H

1271. Vase: Tapestry, Triple Pink Roses, Gold Rim – 4"H

1272. Creamer: Tapestry, Triple Pink Roses, Pinched Spout – 4¼"H

1273. Creamer: Tapestry, Triple Pink Roses, Square Handle (to Tea Set) – 2¾"H

1274. Shoes: Tapestry, Triple Pink Roses, Left and Right, High Top with Original Laces, Very Rare – 3¼"H

Row 4: **1275.** Nut Set: Tapestry, Triple Pink Roses; Very Rare Set, Footed, Master – 3"H x 6"W Small – 1¾"H x 3"W

1276. Relish: Tapestry, Triple Pink Roses, Open Handle, Gold Rim – 8"L x 4"W

1277. Plate: Tapestry, Triple Pink Roses, Gold Rim – 6"D

PAGE 103

Row 1: **1278.** Plate: Tapestry, Portrait Lady, (Large Purple Hat, Right Profile), Gold Scroll Rim, Very Rare – 9½"D

1279. Vase: Tapestry, Portrait Lady, (Large Purple Hat, Right Profile), Bulbous, Stick Spout, Rare – 6"H

1280. Hanging Match Holder: Tapestry, Portrait Lady (Large White Hat, Left Profile) – 4½"H

1281. Vase: Tapestry, Portrait Lady (Large White Hat, Left Profile), Very Rare – 7"H

1282. Dish: Tapestry, Portrait Lady (Large White Hat, Left Profile), Dessert or Sauce Size, Shell and Leaf Mold – 5¾"D

1283. Vase: Tapestry, Portrait Lady (Large White Hat, Left Profile) – 4"H

1284. Powder Jar (with Lid): Tapestry, Portrait Lady (Large Purple Hat, Right Profile), Footed, Rare – 2½"H x 4¼"W

1285. Hatpin Holder: Tapestry, Portrait Lady (Large White Hat, Left Profile), Reticulated Base, Rare – 4½"H

Row 2: **1286.** Vase: Tapestry, Prince and His Lady, Reverse Cone Shape, Gold Rim, Very Rare – 8¾"H

1287. Dresser Tray: Tapestry, Prince and His Lady – 9¾"L x 7"W

1288. Basket: Tapestry, Prince and His Lady, Gold Handle – 6"H x 6½"L

1289. Vase: Tapestry, Portrait Lady (Large Purple Hat, Right Profile), Bulbous, Stick Spout, Very Rare – 8"H

Row 3: **1290.** Creamer: Tapestry, Prince and His Lady, Square Handle – 3¼"H

1291. Vase: Tapestry, Prince and His Lady, Matching Pair – 4¾"H

1292. Hatpin Holder: Tapestry, Prince and His Lady – 5"H

1293. Powder Jar (with Lid): Tapestry, Prince and His Lady, Large Size, Rare – 3½"H x 6"W

Row 4: **1294.** Powder Jar (with Lid): Tapestry, Prince and His Lady, Small Size – 2"H x 3¼"W

1295. Creamer: Tapestry, Prince and His Lady – 2½"H

1296. Powder Jar (with Lid): Tapestry, Prince and His Lady, Medium Size – 2¼"H x 4¼"W

PAGE 104

Row 1: **1297.** Charger Plate: Tapestry, Dark Orange-Gold and Pink Roses, Gold Scroll Rim, Very Rare – 11¼"H

1298. Plate: Tapestry, Pink American Beauty Roses, Gold Scroll Rim – 9½"D

1299. Plate: Tapestry, Pink American Beauty Roses, Shell and Leaf Mold – 7½"D

Row 2: **1300.** Vase: Tapestry, Pink American Beauty Rose – 6"H

1301. Bowl: Tapestry, Pink American Beauty Rose, Shell and Leaf Mold Leaf – 10½"D

1302. Vase: Tapestry, Pink American Beauty Roses, Ornate Handles, Very Rare – 9¼"H

1303. Creamer: Tapestry, Pink American Beauty Roses, Pinched Spout – 4"H

1304. Milk Pitcher: Tapestry, Pink American Beauty Roses, Pinched Spout – 5"H

Row 3: **1305.** Vase: Tapestry, Pink American Beauty Roses, Bulbous, Stick Spout – 4¾"H

1306. Teapot (with Lid): Tapestry, Pink American Beauty Roses, (To Tea Set) – 3¼"H x 6½"L

1307. Cracker Jar (with Lid): Tapestry, Pink American Beauty Roses, Knob Handles – 4¾"H x 6½"W

1308. Vase: Tapestry, Pink American Beauty Roses, Footed, Ruffled Top, with Handles – 4¼"H

Row 4: **1309.** Bowl: Tapestry, Pink American Beauty Roses, Shell and Leaf Mold – 5¾"D

1310. Sugar (with Lid): Tapestry, Pink American Beauty Rose, (To Tea Set) – 3"H

1311. Creamer (To Tea Set): Tapestry, Pink American Beauty Roses (To Tea Set) – 3½"H

1312. Basket: Tapestry, Pink American Beauty Roses, Ruffled Top Handle – 4¾"H x 5"W

ROYAL BAYREUTH TODAY

Our four visits to the Royal Bayreuth factory have been both interesting and educational. As we saw how this well-known porcelain was produced, it made us, as collectors, more appreciative of the heritage of our hobby. We learned that the present workers and management of the Tettau factory are very proud of the excellent quality of their porcelain.

Factory mark used on Royal Bayreuth today.

The village of Tettau lies about one mile from the border that had separated East and West Germany until reunification took place in 1989. Portions of the tall, forbidding barbed wire fence still remained at the time of our last visit in 1993–a grim reminder of the past. The guard towers were once filled with armed soldiers who watched every passing car through binoculars. The towers are now empty and being dismantled. Drab, unpainted buildings on the eastern side, neglected since the division occurred in 1945, are being torn down or restored to their original beauty.

Since Tettau was located on the western side of the division, it enjoyed the post-war progress of West Germany and the European Common Market. Interestingly, a pipeline from the former U.S.S.R. provided the Tettau factory with gas to fire its kilns, but the porcelain factories in the old G.D.R. were forced to use coal because they could not afford the higher cost of gas. The Tettau company began hiring workers from the G.D.R. only a week after German unification. As of 1993, about 25 employees still lived on the eastern side of the old border.

Today, there are three porcelain factories and two glass factories in the village of Tettau. With a population of just 2,000, the village offers about 2,400 job opportunities. Since unification, the Royal Tettau company has also acquired three well-known figurine factories north of Tettau in what was formerly East Germany. These companies, long known for delicate, high-quality work, add a new dimension to Royal Tettau's position in the industry.

Royal Tettau's current market covers Europe, Canada, and the U.S.A. About 80 percent of their goods go to the European Common Market countries, which include France, Germany, Italy, Switzerland, Belgium, Holland, and Great Britain. About 15 percent goes to Sweden and Denmark, three percent to Canada, and even less to the United States.

My husband and I had the privilege of seeing this fine porcelain being made, as we were escorted through the factory by Alfred Herold, head sales director, with the permission of the present director, Werner Weiherer. The immaculate facility is spread out so that each department has a large area to accomplish its part of the procedure.

The special porcelain formula is mixed at a plant 40 km from Tettau. This firm, which is owned by Tettau, specializes in preparing the batches for several porcelain manufacturers. In years past, each porcelain factory mixed their own ingredients, and they would have kept their company's formula under lock and key.

Tettau's special formula consists of approximately 50 percent *kaolin* (a fine white clay that is shipped in from Czechoslovakia and Spain), 25 percent *sand* and 25 percent *feldspar* (a crystalline

Werner Weiherer, present director of Royal Tettau.

Alfred Herold (right), very helpful factory executive and friend through two years of correspondence. Jurgen Laachmann (left) – factory executive and friend.

mineral found in igneous rocks that is formed after cooling and solidifying). The amounts of the ingredients may vary according to the texture desired–for example, the more kaolin, the harder and more translucent the porcelain.

These ingredients are carefully washed, ground, and pulverized before being mixed together as a paste. The water is pressed out of the creamy mass to form plastic cakes, which are stored in low temperature compartments to be aged. When properly aged, they are put into a mixing machine which

Turning machine that molds the various shapes and sizes of wares.

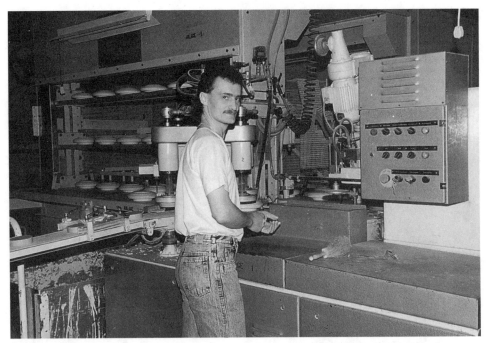

Worker operating "molding" machine.

produces a consistent dough for turning or molding. This material goes to the factory at Tettau where it is stored in long, plastic-covered cylinders until ready for use.

For the past ten years, Tettau has used two molding machines to produce round, flat items such as platters, plates, and saucers. The porcelain is sliced from the cylinders, then pressed into a mold. Each machine is capable of turning out 4,000 items per day. Metal wires gently smooth the edges of each item, which eliminates any need for hand finishing. Previously it required a great number of workers to match the output of these machines.

For objects such as teapots, cups, cream pitchers, and sugar bowls, the "slip" (batch in liquid form) is still poured by hand into the molds. Handles are cast separately three at a time, then glued to cups or bowls before the first firing. These items still require much hand work. We watched as ten women in this department checked for irregularities and cleaned each item by brushing away the excess clay. It is a continual problem to keep the molds clean and useable. Their average life is only about 40 items per mold. Machines have been added to handle larger, heavier items. Unlike the ones used to make the plates, however, these machines add very little to speed production.

Worker brushing and cleaning (by hand) each piece after the handles have been applied.

The factory personnel were very proud of their new casting machine. Tettau was chosen to be the first and only porcelain factory in the whole industry to have this machine. It is only used for large oval items, like platters, and requires only one mold. This device has increased production from 400 to 1000 pieces per day. The operator is a former lieutenant in the East German Army, who sought employment at the time of the unification. Before the machine, this operation required three workers and 250 molds.

After molding and cleaning, the objects are put into the kiln for the first firing at 1000 degrees centigrade for 30 hours. This eliminates all moisture and hardens the items sufficiently for handling. In this state, the porcelain is brittle and porous and can freely absorb the fluid glaze. Tettau uses two kilns for firing, with a third kiln kept as a back up in case of break down. (It takes six weeks to cool, repair, and re-fire a kiln.)

The items are then cooled and passed to the stamping table. If the piece has its design in relief, therefore needing no decorative decals, the trademark is applied with a rubber stamp. At this point, a worker hand dips each

"Casting" or "Mold" department. Worker pouring the 'slip' to form the mold.

New casting machine – Tettau has the only machine of this type used in the porcelain industry.

Mr. Herold showing pieces that are going into one of the three kilns.

piece in glaze. Ingredients in the glaze are like that used for making porcelain, except that more feldspar and other fluxes have been added to promote fusion. In the dipping process, each piece is uniformly covered with glaze.

After glazing, the pieces return to the kiln for a second firing at 1420 degrees centigrade for 36 hours. Some items, such as vases and plaques, are given a third firing at 900 degrees for 24 hours. Products intended to be dishwasher safe are fired at 1200 degrees for up to five days. The end result of this firing process is genuine porcelain–a material that is hard, white, finely textured, translucent, acid-resistant, impervious, low heat conducting, and resonant.

Design room artist – Drawings are made into decals and then applied.

Workers hand cleaning and brushing each piece before it is put into the kiln.

Worker applying rubber stamp to the bottom of the item before it goes to the glazing vat.

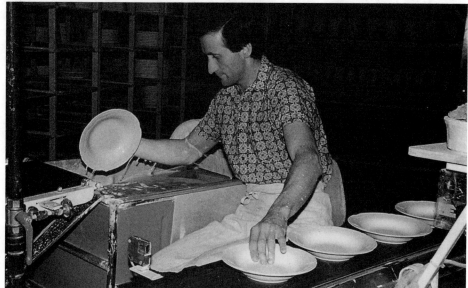

Worker "hand dipping" each piece into the glazing vat before it goes into the kiln.

If pieces have decals for designs or trademarks, these are usually applied with water over the glaze before the third firing. A portion of the decal burns away in the kiln, leaving only the colored design. Sometimes a fourth firing is done at a lower temperature to bring out gold highlights in a design.

Different colors have been used for trademarks and designs, but factory officials say this has no special meaning, as wares cannot be dated on this basis. All Royal Tettau items are marked, except for unused white blanks that might be sold to other porcelain companies.

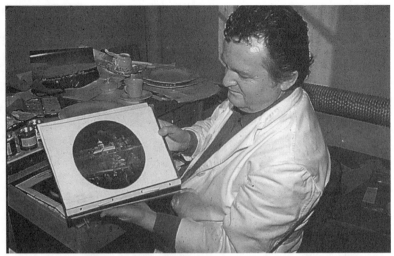

Joseph Newbauer – Artist who has designed the Christmas plates of Tettau.

About twelve women were working in the decal department at the time of our visit. Samples of each piece are kept and marked near the decal station, so that re-orders may be filled at a later date. This insures that later issues are identical in design to the original pieces.

Management at the Tettau factory told us that health-safety standards for porcelain differ from country to country. The United States has the most stringent, followed by Germany and Sweden.

Sales Room...Present day production...

Business street through the village of Tettau, Germany.

The "design" room was really a treat to witness, as we watched three talented artists at their tables creating future designs for Royal Tettau Porcelain. Designs were painted on blanks, much like the way it was done in the 18th century. Each year about 200 new designs are submitted to company officials, but only four or five actually go into production. A representative from another company may view the remaining designs and select one for a "limited edition" offering. The cost of the full production of each design varies from 40,000 to 50,000 deutchmarks.

One of the artists whom we met, Joseph Neeubauer, has designed and created all the Royal Bayreuth Christmas plates. He was very proud to show us the 1993 edition and he gave us a photograph of one of his Christmas plates.

With modernization, Tettau has been able to maintain the same productive level with 200 employees that, before the machines were in use, would have required 600 employees. The company now employs a work force of about 135 women and 65 men. Working hours are 6:30 a.m. to 3:30 p.m. and on Friday, 6:30 a.m. to 12:30 p.m. The early Friday departure gives the workers time to go to nearby cities for shopping, as Tettau is a small village.

Each year there are spring and fall exhibitions in Frankfurt, Germany. Buyers from all over the world gather to preview the new lines from various factories. Also, Royal Bayreuth (Tettau) has sales agents in all common market countries, as well as Canada and the United States. The marketing managers attend a trade fair each year at Milan, Italy. In addition, the Tettau factory has a show room, but it is open to visitors only on Tuesdays.

Archive room in the factory. Very few pieces are on display of the "old" Royal Bayreuth due to the fire 100 years ago.

Each time we visited the factory, we viewed the pieces displayed in the company archives. Of course, these few items do not begin to show the full extent of Royal Bayreuth production. Most examples of the pre-1900 wares were destroyed in the fire of 1897. The items on display were acquired by purchase or donation. The oldest piece in the archives (c. 1800) is what workers called the Straw Pattern (or Chrysanthemum) in "Old Tettau Blue." There is another room at the factory that has samples of many of the items made since 1900.

The staff at the Tettau factory recommended a local history museum in Teltge, Westphalia, Germany where there were several pieces of early Royal Bayreuth. I was aware of this collection and, in fact, had previously written to the director.

"Old Tettau Blue" pattern – Oldest pieces with metal spout (c. 1800) with "T" mark.

"Old Tettau Chrysanthemum" pattern. Circa 1800 with "T" mark.

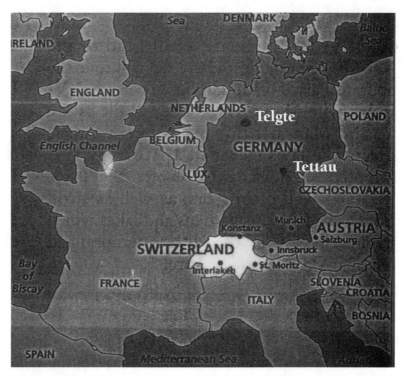

Telgte, Germany – Museum containing "oldest" examples, seven hour drive northwest of Tettau.

141

Telgte, Germany – displaying old "T" examples.

The museum is 450 kilometers northwest of Tettau, near the city of Munster. When we arrived after a seven-hour drive, we asked for directions at the local police station. They kindly escorted us through a narrow one-way street to the museum, called "Heimathaus Munsterland." The building has the characteristic style of an old pastoral barn of the 17th century. It had been restored in 1934 as a place for exhibiting folklore from the Munster area–especially pertaining to peasant culture.

Upon meeting Dr. Thomas Ostendorf, museum director, he recalled the earlier letter that I had sent. He and his assistant, Thomas Schuzann, were eager to show us their collection. We were taken to a room which displayed about 60 pieces of pre-1830 Royal Bayreuth. They were all marked with the first and oldest "T" mark. Dr. Ostendorf stated that the Telgte area served as a Royal Tettau distribution center from 1830-1840. Studying these pieces helped us confirm the information that we had received at Tettau.

Two coffee pots with lids illustrate typical early Royal Bayreuth wares. Both date to the first half of the 19th century and have painted decorations under the glaze. One is a large pot in the old Meissen style with a pear-shaped body, a light base, short neck, curved metal spout, and sturdy handle. The hand-painted decoration is in the "Old Tettau Blue" pattern. The second pot has an egg-shaped body on a base and a button-top lid. The body has a short neck and slightly enlarged mouth. Both body and spout on the neck are ribbed. The curved handle ends in a point. The painted decoration is in the "Old Tettau Chrysanthemum" pattern.

Today, the Royal Bayreuth factory produces beautiful tableware of all kinds, as well as novelty pieces. We collectors of the beautiful and unique "old" Royal Bayreuth porcelain should be proud to know that our pieces came from a factory with a rich and varied history.

RECORD OF OWNERSHIP AND DIRECTORS

The Royal Tettau Porcelain Factory
Porcelain Factory Tettau, Ltd.

1794 – One document serves to prove the establishment by the King's royal decree on December 28, 1794 of the Royal Tettau Porcelain Factory. In it, the firm's founder, Georg Christian Friedemann Greiner from Kloster (Convent) Veilsdorf near Coburg, and a Coburg citizen, the merchant Johann Friedrich Paul Schmidt, were given the right by royal decree to establish an "esteemed porcelain factory in the sub-district (county) of Lauenstein." The signers of this decree were the sovereign of Prussia, King Friedrich Wilhelm II and his Minister, Prince Hardenberg.

1817 – The Tettau factory was inherited by the youngest son (Balthasar) of the founder. The most notable high point of Tettau porcelain production was during the period of the Biedermeier Style (1810 - 1840). Written, printed, or word of mouth information about the destiny of the Tettau porcelain factory from then until 1921 is incomplete. The Tettau porcelain factory was in the possession of the Greiner family until 1852.

1852 – It was in the possession of Otto Hausler from Breslau.

1857 – Hausler brought Ferdinand Klaus into the firm as a partner.

1866 - 1879 – The owners were Wilhelm Sontag and Karl Birkner.

1879 - 1902 – Karl Birkner and L. Maisel were the sole owners.

1897 – After the factory burned down, Karl Birkner constructed a significantly larger factory complex.

1902 - 1915 – The factory was controlled and directed by the firm "Sontag & Sons, Ltd.". The fire which had destroyed the original factory also destroyed all those things of significance (records and files) as pertains to the history of the factory

1915 – The **old** porcelain factory (as differentiated from the **new** factory founded in 1904) was converted into a public stock company.

1917 – The Quartz Sand factory Bauer and Company in Weissenbrunn, was acquired.

1920 – The factory in Mainleus was converted to the production of electro-technical porcelain.

1938 – Transfer (trade) of the Mainleus porcelain factory as part of the purchase of the Hochstadt Porcelain Factory.

1940 – Sale of the Hochstadt Porcelain Factory to the Siemens Corporation.

Today, the factory is a modern industrial enterprise which is well regarded by neighboring businesses. At one time it provided its workers with housing and small garden plots.

DIRECTORS OF THE COMPANY

1915	– 1916	–	Jahne
1916	– 1918	–	Grimm. Schomburg and Pitsch
1918	– 1939	–	Max Wunderlich
1939	– 1947	–	Max Wunderlich (trusteeship)
1947	– 1958	–	Max Wunderlich
1958	– 1968	–	Strossenreuther
1968	– 1989	–	Helmut Weichler
1989	–		Werner Weiherer

BIBLIOGRAPHY

Bagdade, Susan and Al. *Warman's English and Continental Pottery and Porcelain: An Illustrated Price Guide.* Willow Grove, Pa.: Warman Publishing Co., Inc., 1987.

Cameron, Elisabeth. *Encyclopedia of Pottery and Porcelain 1800-1960.* New York: Facts on File Publications, 1986.

Danckert, Ludwig. *Handbuch des Europäischen Porzellans.* München: Prestel Verlag, 1954.

Dees, Dr. K. Otto. *Die Geschichte der Porzellanfabrik zu Tettau und die Beziehungen Alexander v. Humboldts zur Porzellanindustrie.* Saalfeld i. Thür., 1921.

Haggar, Reginald G. *The Concise Encyclopedia of Continental Pottery and Porcelain.* New York: Hawthorn Books, Inc., 1960.

Klingenbrunn, Marietta. *Deutsche Porzellanmarken von 1708 bis heute.* Augsburg: Battenberg Verlag, 1990.

Poche, Emanuel. *Porzellan-marken aus Aller Welt.* Werner Dausien, 1975.

Raines, Joan and Marvin. *A Guide to Royal Bayreuth Figurals.* Self published, 1973.

Raines, Joan and Marvin. *A Guide to Royal Bayreuth Figurals, Book 2.* Self published, 1977.

Rontgen, Robert E. *Marks on German, Bohemian and Austrian Porcelain 1710 to the Present.* Exton, Pa.: Schiffer Publishing Ltd., 1981.

Salley, Virginia Sutton and George H. *Royal Bayreuth China.* Self published, 1969.

Tischert, Hans. "Königl. priv. Porzellanfabrik Tettau Aktiengesellschaft." *Statten Deutscher Arbeit, Band X.* Berlin, circa 1920, pp. 72-79.

von Waltraut Schneiderhahl. *175 Jahre Königlich Privilegierte Porzellanfabrik Tettau.* Nurnberg, 1969.

Ware, George W. *German and Austrian Porcelain.* New York: Crown Publishers, Inc., 1963.

Wojciechowski, Kathy. "Nippon Imitated Royal Bayreuth's Rose Tapestry Technique." *New York-Pennsylvania Collector,* November 1992, p.14

INDEX

CRACKER JARS:
Scenic – 38
Figural – 294, 399, 475, 507, 536, 538, 583
Tapestry – 1168, 1227, 1307.

CREAMERS:
Scenic – 10, 15, 27, 28, 43, 44, 80, 83, 84, 85, 87, 91, 113, 123
Figural – 258, 263, 265, 268, 270, 274, 289, 291, 316, 317, 319, 351, 361, 362, 365, 366, 371, 378, 386, 389, 394, 404, 415, 416, 417, 418, 419, 428, 440, 442, 448, 459, 460, 466, 486, 489, 504, 510, 523, 528, 539, 549, 554, 559, 562, 589, 593, 594, 598, 606, 607, 608, 610, 613, 616, 618, 625, 628, 630 633, 636, 637, 638, 639, 652, 654, 655, 660, 662, 663, 664, 665, 666, 670, 673 674, 680, 681, 683, 687, 690, 691, 699, 701, 705, 706, 711, 712, 718, 719, 722, 723, 724, 726, 728, 729, 731, 732, 733, 734, 735, 738, 742, 743, 744, 747, 749, 750, 757, 765, 775, 790, 798, 814, 815, 816, 817, 818, 821, 824, 827, 844, 849, 853, 857, 860, 867, 872, 875, 881, 902, 913, 914
Tapestry – 921, 927, 947, 963, 978, 982, 1013, 1019, 1037, 1038, 1056, 1060, 1072, 1074, 1095, 1098, 1112, 1115, 1118, 1125, 1131, 1151, 1153, 1159, 1165, 1172, 1181, 1209, 1229, 1243, 1244, 1254, 1267, 1272, 1273, 1290, 1295, 1303, 1311.

CUP AND SAUCERS:
89.
Scenic – 155, 156, 157, 158
Figural – 325, 326, 354, 355, 391, 430, 433, 435, 531, 789, 797
Tapestry – 924.

DEMITASSE CUP OR SAUCER:
Figural – 266, 267, 285, 332, 376, 392, 425, 454, 463, 483, 484, 544, 574, 587, 793, 896, 897.

DESK SET:
Scenic – 168, 169, 170, 171, 172, 173, 174 175, 176.

DISHES:
Figural – 545, 552

Tapestry – 957, 958, 959, 961, 1004, 1150, 1188, 1195, 1218, 1222, 1282.

DRESSER SET:
Scenic – 242 to 249, 250 to 254.

DRESSER TRAY:
Scenic – 243, 251
Figural – 754, 870
Tapestry – 938, 955, 1000, 1024, 1042, 1058, 1109, 1111, 1169, 1194, 1248, 1261, 1287.

EWERS:
Tapestry – 925, 975, 1034, 1066, 1107, 1212.

GRAVY BOAT (with underplate):
Figural – 488, 513.

HAIR RECEIVERS:
Scenic – 59, 119, 249, 253
Figural – 277, 413
Tapestry – 920, 941, 992, 1047, 1079, 1088, 1196, 1208, 1249.

HAT PIN HOLDERS:
Scenic – 73, 177, 178, 179, 180, 181, 182, 183, 184, 185, 186, 187, 188, 189, 190, 191, 192, 193, 194, 195, 196, 197, 198, 199, 200, 201, 202, 203, 204, 205, 206, 207, 208, 209, 210, 211, 212, 213, 214, 215, 216, 217, 218, 219, 220, 221, 222, 1071
Figural – 223, 224, 225, 226, 227, 228, 229, 230, 231, 232, 233, 234, 235, 236, 237, 238, 239, 240, 241, 242, 250, 252, 288, 311, 570, 647, 702, 751
Tapestry – 946, 998, 1048, 1071, 1097, 1246, 1285, 1292.

INKWELLS:
Scenic – 30, 171, 173, 176
Figural – 777.

LADIES PURSE (or bag):
578.

LADIES:
Figural – 281, 305, 518.

LEMONADE PITCHERS:
Scenic – 6, 62
Figural – 445, 490, 635, 677, 715, 904, 911
Tapestry – 1170.

LETTER HOLDER:
Scenic – 170.

LOVING CUP:
Scenic – 68, 79.

MARMALADE JAR:
Figural – 456, 543, 586.

MATCH HOLDERS:
Scenic – 13, 94, 95, 114, 175
Figural – 382, 393, 397, 668, 717, 737, 769,
  783, 792, 796, 835, 836, 840, 847, 876,
  877, 901, 908, 918
Tapestry – 983, 1018, 1059, 1101, 1106, 1126
  1127, 1166, 1230, 1280.

MAYONNAISE SET:
Figural – 411.

MILK PITCHERS:
Scenic – 7, 9, 11, 20, 21, 22, 23, 74, 104, 105,
  106, 115, 124, 164, 165
Figural – 262, 264, 310, 352, 358, 360, 367,
  408, 421, 427, 436 444, 446, 458, 481, 491,
  497, 503, 521, 535, 553, 560, 572, 580, 592,
  597, 599, 602, 611, 615, 619, 621, 624, 627,
  631, 642, 643, 651, 653, 658, 661, 672, 675,
  679, 682, 689, 694, 697, 698, 703, 707, 710,
  713, 720, 725, 727, 730, 745, 746, 764, 774,
  791, 799, 800, 801, 813, 826, 845, 852, 856,
  861, 873, 885, 905, 906, 907, 915, 916
Tapestry – 931, 948, 971, 1005, 1021, 1033,
  1084, 1154, 1255, 1268, 1304.

MINIATURES:
Coal Hod or Scuttle: Scenic – 13
Tapestry – 926, 985, 1114, 1152, 1211.
Ewer: Tapestry – 925, 975, 1212.
Pitchers: Tapestry – 1070, 1073, 1214.
Sofa: Tapestry – 1075
Vase: Scenic – 93, 96, 120, 121, 154
Tapestry – 1217

Watering Can: Tapestry – 1031, 1214, 1215,
  1216.

MUGS:
Figural – 772, 784, 828, 882, 884
Tapestry – 962, 1184.

MUSTARD POTS:
Scenic – 112
Figural – 257, 300, 331, 429, 453, 461, 464,
  494, 512, 515, 529, 541, 547, 582.

NAPPY:
Scenic – 41, 61
Figural – 282, 321, 322, 370
Tapestry – 1022, 1064, 1119, 1128, 1137,
  1210.

NUT OR MINT SET (or dish):
Scenic – 77
Figural – 276, 297, 298, 323, 341, 342, 349
  381, 387
Tapestry – 1231, 1275.

PAPER WEIGHT:
Scenic – 172.

PEN and PENCIL TRAY:
Scenic – 174.

PICTURE FRAME:
Scenic – 8
Tapestry – 1080, 1081.

PIN BOX (or Trinket Box):
Scenic – 246, 248
Tapestry – 1001, 1002, 1008, 1020, 1055,
  1078, 1086, 1121, 1132, 1179, 1200,
  1258.

PIN CUSHION:
Figural – 786
Tapestry – 1005.

PIN TRAY:
Scenic – 29
Figural – 761
Tapestry – 1199.

PIPE REST:
Figural – 641, 834, 843.

PLANTER: (or Flower Pots):
Figural – 259, 275, 283, 780
Tapestry – 922, 945, 1012, 1051, 1062,
   1093, 1189, 1232, 1245, 1269.

PLATES:
Scenic – 1, 3, 18, 34, 72, 75, 78, 99, 101, 103,
   139, 140, 141, 142, 143, 144, 145, 146, 148,
   162
Figural – 255, 273, 292, 309, 318, 327, 330,
   344, 345, 346, 347, 348, 350, 363, 455,
   465, 473, 476, 493, 537
Tapestry – 40, 933, 934, 952, 954, 966, 969,
   972, 1023, 1082, 1123, 1148, 1235, 1238,
   1239, 1262, 1263, 1264, 1277, 1278, 1297,
   1298, 1299.

WALL PLAQUE:
Scenic – 5, 160.

POWDER JARS:
Scenic – 245, 254
Figural – 833
Tapestry – 943, 964, 965, 991, 1003, 1040,
   1117, 1129, 1161, 1162, 1177, 1187, 1197,
   1234, 1247, 1284, 1293, 1294, 1296.

RELISH DISH:
Scenic – 45
Figural – 269, 380, 412, 795
Tapestry – 1063, 1233, 1237, 1276.

RING HOLDER (Ring Tree):
Tapestry – 1045, 1139, 1140.

SALT and PEPPER SHAKERS:
Scenic – 16, 48, 50
Figural – 256, 304, 333, 335, 336, 337, 340,
   364, 374, 424, 431, 469, 470, 471, 487,
   509, 516, 532, 534, 542, 550, 561, 563,
   564, 565, 566, 567, 568, 569, 584, 778,
   838, 864, 889
Tapestry – 1077, 1100, 1226.

SALT DIP:
Figural – 280, 284, 299, 324, 339, 434, 546.

SCUTTLE MUGS:
Scenic – 26.

SHAVING MUG:
Figural – 784.

SHOES:
804, 805, 806, 807, 808, 809, 810, 811, 819,
   820, 822, 823, 928, 942, 997, 1006, 1090,
   1146, 1202, 1252, 1253, 1274.

STAMP BOX:
Scenic – 168
Figural – 575
Tapestry – 1030.

STICK PIN HOLDER:
Scenic – 247.

STRING HOLDER:
Figural – 620.

SUGAR BOWLS:
Scenic – 86, 90, 117
Figural – 272, 301, 306, 320, 328, 329, 372,
   377, 385, 405, 439, 462, 485, 495, 500,
   508, 525, 527, 540, 555, 556, 576, 588,
   622, 684, 716, 766, 785, 787, 886, 887,
   890, 898
Tapestry – 1173, 1198, 1228, 1310.

SUGAR SHAKER:
Tapestry – 1052.

SYRUP:
Figural – 782.

TANKARD:
Scenic – 2, 65, 100.

TEA POT:
Scenic – 14, 52, 53, 54, 55, 56, 88, 92, 116
Figural – 260, 302, 307, 451, 472, 482, 496
499, 501, 519, 590
Tapestry – 956, 983, 1176, 1306.

TEA STRAINER:
Figural – 279, 303, 409, 410.

TODDY SET or CUP:
Figural – 797.

TOOTHBRUSH HOLDER:
Tapestry – 999, 1039, 1185, 1212.

TOOTHPICK HOLDERS:
Scenic – 24, 42, 46,
Figural – 293, 406, 432, 514, 788, 837, 858, 859, 863, 865, 899
Tapestry – 110, 111, 977, 984, 987, 1016, 1044, 1054, 1099, 1160, 1167, 1174, 1175, 1213, 1259, 1260.

TRAY:
Figural – 384.

TUMBLERS:
Tapestry – 923, 1017, 1032.

VASES:
Scenic – 19, 39, 47, 63, 70, 93, 96, 118, 120, 121, 154
Figural – 755, 758
Tapestry – 97, 930, 935, 936, 944, 951, 967, 968, 973, 974, 976, 980, 981, 986, 988, 989, 990, 999, 1010, 1015, 1025, 1027, 1028, 1035, 1036, 1039, 1046, 1057, 1068, 1069, 1085, 1089, 1104, 1108, 1110, 1113, 1116, 1120, 1122, 1130, 1134, 1135, 1136, 1142, 1147, 1149, 1155, 1156, 1157, 1158, 1163, 1164, 1180, 1182, 1185, 1190, 1192, 1193, 1201, 1203, 1204, 1205, 1206, 1207, 1217, 1219, 1220, 1221, 1240, 1241, 1250, 1271, 1279, 1281, 1283, 1286, 1289, 1291, 1300, 1302, 1305, 1308.

WALL MATCH HOLDERS:
Figural – 379

WALL VASE or POCKET:
Figural – 315, 338, 343, 403, 585, 756, 912
Tapestry – 950, 1191, 1218.

WATERING CAN:
Tapestry – 1031, 1214, 1215, 1216.

WATER PITCHERS:
Floral – 49
Scenic– 109
Figural – 290, 359, 400, 422, 423, 426, 443, 447, 457, 474, 492, 498, 502, 505, 520, 533, 548, 571, 579, 591, 595, 596, 600, 601, 603, 605, 609, 612, 617, 623, 626, 629, 632, 634, 650, 659, 669, 671, 676, 678, 685, 686, 688, 695, 696, 704, 708, 709, 714, 721, 739, 741, 763, 773, 802, 825, 846, 850, 854, 855, 871, 910.
Tapestry – 937, 939, 1014, 1026, 1083.